Running

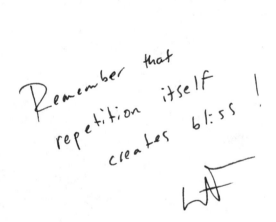

Remember that
repetition itself
creates bliss !

Practices

A series edited by Margret Grebowicz

Running

Lindsey A. Freeman

ILLUSTRATIONS BY HAZEL MEYER

DUKE UNIVERSITY PRESS
Durham and London
2023

© 2023 DUKE UNIVERSITY PRESS
Printed in the United States of America on acid-free paper ∞
Designed by A. Mattson Gallagher
Typeset in Untitled Serif and General Sans
by Copperline Book Services

Library of Congress Cataloging-in-Publication Data
Names: Freeman, Lindsey A., author.
Title: Running / Lindsey A. Freeman.
Other titles: Practices.
Description: Durham : Duke University Press, 2023. | Series: Practices
Identifiers: LCCN 2022035503 (print)
LCCN 2022035504 (ebook)
ISBN 9781478017011 (hardcover)
ISBN 9781478019657 (paperback)
ISBN 9781478024286 (ebook)
Subjects: LCSH: Running—Social aspects. | Running—Physiological
aspects. | Running—Psychological aspects. | Queer theory. | Feminist
theory. | BISAC: SPORTS & RECREATION / Running & Jogging
Classification: LCC GV1061 .F74 2023 (print) | LCC GV1061 (ebook) |
DDC 796.42—dc23/eng/20220811
LC record available at https://lccn.loc.gov/2022035503
LC ebook record available at https://lccn.loc.gov/2022035504

Cover text handwritten by Lindsey A. Freeman.

for Jessi

CONTENTS

.

ACKNOWLEDGMENTS

This book was written during weird and anxious times. The handbook was both my project and my company through the COVID global pandemic, the Russian invasion of Ukraine, and a variety of personal struggles. In order to keep going, sometimes I needed my writing and running friends to give me a lift and to shake me out of my pain cave. Thanks to Amanda Watson, Coleman Nye, Cait McKinney, and Andrea Actis, who got behind the seriousness. Karen Engle read countless drafts, listened to excited talk about the minutiae of running, and believed in this project, even when I was unsure how it would all fit together. Lauren Berlant, Ann Cvetkovich, Craig Campbell, Randy Lewis, Marina Peterson, and Katie Stewart from my Public Feelings writing group listened to and shared feedback on several sections in their early stages and helped them to loop smoother, and with better form.

Thank you as well to my research assistants Ileanna Cheladyn, Abu Fakhri, and Marina Khonina. And to the Department of Sociology and Anthropology at Simon Fraser University for the leave from teaching that made my almost total immersion in the research and writing of this book possible.

In gratitude for Jane Andersen and Nancy Scola, who always pick me up when I'm run over. For Leslie Bernstein, Mo Botton, Monica Brannon, Rachel Daniell, Linsey Ly, Asifa Malik, Ben Neinass, Lauren Packard, and everyone who was there for me in the aftermath of the CR-V. To Tara Lohan and Megamo Nesbit for the friendship and the place to rest my swollen knee when I was doing something like research. And to my doctor Sara Forsyth, physios Jessica (Owen) Reigh and Paul Biazey, chiro Dr. Vivien Chiu, and RMT Nic Taggart for helping to keep me running despite all the big and little ways my body has failed to hold up against my ragged will. To the Black Lodge Running Club, especially Boback, Jessi, Radar, and Zazie (even though she mostly stayed in the car), thank you for the Saturday long runs and the camaraderie.

To Hazel Meyer, for the drawings and attention to style, you are a dream collaborator. And to the whole editorial team at Duke University Press, especially Elizabeth Ault and Ben Kossak. I was deeply moved by the care taken with my manuscript by the peer reviewers and everyone this handbook encountered on its way to being itself. And without the acumen, generosity, and tenacity of the series editor, Margret Grebowicz, this handbook simply wouldn't be.

And to Jessi Lee Jackson, for always believing in me and for always thinking I'm faster than I am, let's keep living in our montage.

Finally, to all the runners, this book is a nod to you, a little wave in advance for when I see you out there in all the weathers and up all the hills.

Introduction

I was born during the late twentieth-century American jog-ging boom. My family was part of the newly distance-obsessed masses running through the 1980s in tall socks, waffle-soled shoes, and short shorts. We kissed the roads, tracks, and trails of East Tennessee with Brookses, New Balances, and Nikes adorn-ing our feet. As young as five, I ran 5K and 10K races, alongside my parents, collecting T-shirts that fit more like knee-length dresses and trophies topped with golden shapely women whose bodies bore no resemblance to mine. On Sundays, my parents would drive me to the high school track, where I would run lap after lap, timing my splits and miles. I wrote these numbers down in a little notebook, like a pint-size bookie taking bets on myself. I was carefully tracking my progress and dreaming of hitting a personal best or a "PB," as we runners call them.[1]

Most children run spontaneously and freely, but I trained. Before I was allowed to run free in the neighborhood by my-self, I created running loops around the yard, jumping over the

ivy that lined the sidewalk, weaving in and out of the dogwood trees, and giving a high five to the waxy-leaved magnolia as I zipped by. I did hill work, sprinting up the big slope behind the house and jogging slowly back down to touch the fence covered in honeysuckle, licking the sweet nectar from the blossom stems as a reward before racing back up again. I ran countless miniature laps around the cul-de-sac at the end of my street, until I became dizzy. I could have been a tough, tiny contender for the type of "last man standing" backyard ultraraces that are held now: those races where competitors make small circuitous routes over and over, until there is only one runner remaining.[2]

For as long as I can remember, running has been something I do in an earnest and serious way, which is how I do everything I love.

Despite running nearly all my life, I am not an exceptional or elite athlete. I would describe myself as an OK runner. I have set two track records in competition: one in the 800 meters in college and the other for the mile in middle school. I am unlikely to set any more, outside of PBs, and even those seem improbable with my growing collection of tendonitises, but I hold out hope. The last race I ran was a half-marathon in the small coastal city of Anacortes, Washington. When I finished, I had a flush of pride because I thought I might have won my age-group. As it turns out, the runner who beat me was so far ahead that I never even saw her. Half-marathon and marathon racing are full of moments like these that don't quite register as humiliations, because no matter what, I've gone the distance.

I'm sure that this feeling manifests after longer races too, in the aftermath of ultramarathons of 50K, 50 miles, 100K, 100 miles, and more (always already more), but I haven't experienced this feeling of ultracompletion . . . yet.

While setting records certainly ferries pleasure, what I love most about running is the way it allows me to make time and space for being in a body feeling my way through a landscape and my own thoughts. When running, I'm not asking myself to be anything other than a runner, a human animal breathing, covering distance, briefly flying, while maintaining a sense for the shifting ground. When I find a rhythm, I can let go, and feelings and thoughts come in waves; it is not unlike dreaming. Running (although not racing) can be freedom from pronouns and peer review.[3] What a relief sometimes, to simply be a person, temporarily shaking loose.

This is not to say that the space of running is a utopia; a variety of mean and terrible things can interrupt even the best run, snap a runner right out of their flow. There are accidents and injuries; dogs that want a piece of you; people on the street and in vehicles who scrutinize bodies, gender police, racially harass, intimidate, and worse. It is puzzling to me, but the very act of seeing someone running seems to trigger rage in a large swath of humanity.

Many years ago, my white middle-aged father was shot with a paint gun while jogging alongside the highway, turning the chest of his white T-shirt a bright crimson. We suspected that the boys who shot him from a minivan, whose wide door they swung open with verve, were my brother's friends, but it might not have been personal; it may be that they just saw a lone runner as an easy target.

I do not know many runners who have not had something hurled at them through the window of a passing car. I have been hit with misogynist insults, gay slurs, ripe peaches, half-full beer cans, and once a fuzzy, red Tickle Me Elmo doll. Men in pickup trucks, in luxury sedans, and on bicycles have ridden alongside me, letting me know they could do anything they wanted to my running body, vulnerable in shorts on the side of the road. Sometimes these men let me know that they saw my body as a feminine one, other times a queer one, and occasionally both.

The murder of Ahmaud Arbery is on my mind too as I write this handbook. I have been thinking of the frightening rage of those three white men who felt that a Black man had no business in their neighborhood. I have been thinking of the gross injustice that many people fear being assaulted or murdered for doing such a simple thing as running.

The release found in running comes from a desire to touch something beyond or within yourself that is difficult to access when still. To run is to move and be moved. This is why it is vital that everyone have access to spaces for running. The ability to enter these spaces, material and immaterial, is what makes it possible to be present for the beautiful and unusual experiences that can emerge from repetition, and from the combination of preparation and chance. These experiences can exceed your imagination; they can shift your sense of what you thought you knew. That the touching and pleasurable spaces of running can be accessed more easily and freely by some runners than others is yet another deep unfairness of our world.

Despite the hostility and violence—the body, gender, racial, social, and spatial boundary policing that runners sometimes receive, and receive unevenly—I still believe that running allows for a space of freedom. It freaks me out to use such a lofty and loaded word as *freedom*, but I'm at my most effusive and sincere when I write about sporting.[4]

Although I have always been drawn to the practice of running, I often feel distant from its popular representations. I come to running culture, as I do with most things, at a slant. I do not often or easily find a sense of queer possibility in most popular books, magazines, or films about running, and it is increasingly difficult to find athletic clothes that both fit my body and match my gender. Each decade seems to bring a narrowing in the options available to athletes who run in clothes purchased from the women's section of sports shops. When I enter these spaces, I often leave confused, having bought nothing and wondering why running clothes need so many cutouts in the thighs, open backs, and spaghetti string tops. I am not opposed to these styles for those who want them, but I wish that there were more options for those of us who don't. Still, I feel a capaciousness in the practice of running itself. I know I'm not alone in this and that there are a lot of us running in the gap between our practices and our desires, our abilities to kit ourselves out in what feels good, and in the representations of what we see in print and through images of others supposedly doing what we do.

Running can be a method and a genre, but it is always laced to the feet of those who carry it. I have not found my pacer among the authors of the dozens of racing memoirs I've read or my ideal pack to train with through the collection of running handbooks I've amassed. Although I have been drawn in by their covers and enthusiasm since I was a kid, poring over the handbooks my parents had lying around featuring images of strong, ropey running legs and promises to address elusive categories like "being," "innerspaces," and "the zen of running," I have not found kinship.[5] While reading popular books about running, I have often been stopped in my tracks midsentence by categories I have come to think of as "weird misogyny," "out-of-the-blue anti-queerness," "casual racism," and "strange essentialisms." When I'm moving through otherwise banal paragraphs, these moments hit me unexpectedly, like an object hurled from a moving car as I run along the road, but they can sting more because I have approached these books willingly; I have come a distance to meet their phrases on the page, paid money for the experience, and expended energy; and I have done so because I love running. As a reader of these books, I'm looking for something, to gain new knowledge—technical or emotional—to experience a world, to touch and be touched by a space of running. Getting struck by these moments of misalignment with the words on the page leaves me angry, disappointed, and longing for another kind of runner's world.

I learned from all my queer punk heroes and heroines who came before, if you don't like the songs on the radio, start your own band, and if you don't like the glossy magazines that pretend you and those you love don't exist, make a zine for your community—do it yourself—and so I wrote the running handbook I couldn't find. Feminist and queer writers require new literary styles to hold us: running is the genre I'm working in now. We also need to make adjustments to old forms that cause us injury, so I wrote this handbook first in running and then translated it to language that works on the page.

Running is always about more than running. When writing about running, the author's way of seeing and modes of being in the world are inevitably folded in. What has been missing for me in most of the running books I've read is a poetics of practice and a resonant theory of running that is not overly confident in what it means to run. Beginning in the seventeenth century, handbooks have traveled under the phrase *vade mecum*, from the Latin meaning "go with me." The meaning is twofold: the first is that the author should be a guide, and the second is that handbooks are designed to move. They should feel good to hold and slip easily into a tote bag or running vest. They should make practices legible and inhabitable: they shouldn't weigh you down. Cousins to manuals, but with more of a personal touch, handbooks separate themselves from the dry books of operation that come in the glove compartment of a new car. At their best they are an invitation to a practice and are thoughtful about form. The kind of handbooks I like contain helpful advice, along with prompts for creativity; they have an emphasis on style rather than an insistence on a mechanical correctness; and they are oriented toward possibility instead of being simply a compendium of rules.

There is always an element of memoir in running handbooks, with the goal of giving a sense of who is behind the paragraphs written to move the reader, and I have kept that convention. Through writing about my practice, I discovered something akin to what Haruki Murakami documents in *What I Talk about When I Talk about Running*, which is that "writing honestly about running and writing honestly about myself are really the same thing."[6] Memoir functions as both a research method and a window into an individual practice, but the sec-

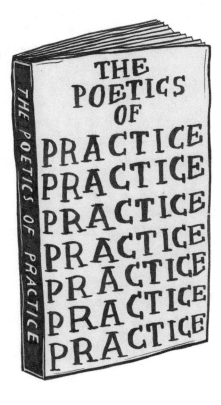

tions of personal history aren't only meant to be a description of what's particular about my running. They are also invitations— openings—to think about your own practices.[7]

Throughout the handbook, I repeatedly turn to artists, poets, queer theorists, and writers, those I think of as my front-runners in theories of love and touch, and whose attention to form and style moves me to make sentences. Roland Barthes's *A Lover's Discourse*, a queer endurance project if there ever was one, has often been a handbook for me when tormented or enchanted by love. With this project I move the object of affection from a person to the practice of running and find that Barthes's formulations resonate just as strongly.[8] I'm especially moved by how he compares the lover to an athlete who strains and struggles and exhausts themselves.[9] In this handbook I'm collapsing the comparison and taking up a hybrid identity, the lover and the athlete, in one freckled body in hot pursuit of what running is and can be. I feel encouraged in this approach through the words of the Scottish writer and Highlands hiker Nan Shepard, who in the foreword to *The Living Mountain*, a book about her endurance practice of hiking in the Cairngorms, writes: "Love pursued with fervor is one of the roads to knowledge."[10]

Running is a durational act, which at its most simple is about time and timing, and about a body (or bodies) moving at pace through space. By developing a practice and doing this simple thing over and over, you learn things about your body and your personality; the bodies and personalities of those you run with; and the textures, surfaces, and atmospheres you run in and through. Following Stefano Harney and Fred Moten, I want to think about the practice of running as a somesthetic space of "hapticality, or love," where hapticality is a capacity for feeling, "a way of feeling through others" and "a feel for others feeling you."[11] So often running is thought of as a solitary practice, but it is also a space full of the potential for connection, and for the kind of beautiful formlessness of friendship that can be a way of life if you let it.[12]

In the essay "Love, a Queer Feeling," Lauren Berlant writes that love creates "an environment of touch . . . that you make so that there is something to which you turn and return."[13] Berlant is not writing about running, but still those words feel like something I can run with. While writing this handbook, I thought about the spaces of touch that running creates. I turned and returned to Berlant to touch a space of queer theory, and as I continue to go through the miles, lines from their essay zip through my "runner-brain" as part of the cadence of my thinking.[14]

The practice of running always exceeds its normative and institutional forms, even when exercising in and through those forms, such as organized marathons, track meets, and the Olympics. To be in excess of institutions, the habitual, the self, identity, pronouns, and/or the body requires stretching. I want to think of stretching in terms of desire and as an increased capacity for feeling. Following Barthes, I see stretching as a form of self-extension that reaches out toward someone or something and as a gesture or a practice that has the potential to "baffle paradigms." Stretching can be a question, a going out on a limb to offer an invitation that pulls up a potential moment of contact, which can be as subtle as a barely perceptible wink or as overt as a grasping for another's hand. Stretching can also be an answer to a question, a response to someone or something else's extension, a reaching toward possibility. It can open you up to a desire you didn't know you had or a connection you never imagined.[15] Stretching is a start to creating environments of touch that you can turn and return to, and a repeated action that allows you to keep touching spaces that feel good.

Running is a handbook that is made possible through friendship, community, and practices stretching toward each other. Alongside the sentences I've written about running are drawings by Hazel Meyer. This collaboration is a direct manifestation of the queer and feminist sporting worlds that shaped me as a runner and a writer. Meyer's body of work—including past and current projects and performances such as *Muscle Panic*, *Walls to the Ball*, and *Witness Fitness*—is built around engagement with feminist and queer aesthetics and histories of athletics. Her strengths as an artist and a documenter of queer and feminist cultures augment my writing, as Hazel and I stretch to meet each other in these pages.

This small queer handbook is not likely to make you a better runner, but if it does, full credit lies with you. *Running* is ultimately a stretch, an invitation to think about what it means to have a regular practice and to run through things at whatever pace, legging it out the best you can with heart and style. There are stories of races here too, and of training for them. These stories are chosen to give a sense of a running life, but they are only a small part of what it means to run. I'm more invested in honoring the work of daily practice, by making visible and beautiful the sometimes weird experiences of running in and of itself. In the following pages, you won't find arguments that humans were made to run or born to run either barefoot or with the most high-tech materials ever imagined strapped to our feet. I'm not convinced that humans were born to do anything in particular, which is part of what makes the things we choose to do carry meaning. To find kinship in this handbook, you don't need to be a runner, a sporting person, or even a writer. You must simply allow for the possibility that logging mile after mile can lead you to places and things you didn't expect, and to consider that running can be an act of love and a means toward contact. Let's keep running. You've already started. *Vade mecum.*

Stride—Form—Cadence—Pace

Each move forward is an assemblage of gestures, a stride. Strides tend to come together, collating into a moving pattern that can be recognized: as form. Form is the series of shapes a runner makes with their body as they move around a track or through a landscape. Form can be witnessed in the limbs, gleaned by a footfall, glimpsed by the position of the head, and heard through the rhythm of steps. When form is heard, it is called by runners "cadence." Cadence comes from the Italian word *cadenza*, meaning "metrical beat." And before *cadenza*, there was the Latin word *cadere*, which means "to fall." Running cadence is the sound of a moving form touching the ground, falling over and over again, forming a score for each run. This score can be heard, but it is also felt through the body of the runner, lighting up their haptic sense. Running is an expression of form in time, what can also be called "rhythm." The rhythm of running is not necessarily even or always pleasing, although as runners we strive for this.

I dream of opening up the temporality in my cadence to recognize what is holding me back. I want to go into slo-mo or to press pause again and again in order to break my form into its parts, so I can see bad patterns emerge. I want to undo these patterns, to disassemble and reorganize them, so that a transformation of my form can take hold. I know that I can do this, and have done this, that people have watched me run on a track, on the grass, on a treadmill. My form has been scrutinized live and taped, by my college track coach, when I was buying shoes at specialty running stores, and at the office of a "primal health" coach, but there is still a fantasy of seeing something else, something technologies, salespeople, and coaches haven't noticed, something between my form being hardwired or honky-tonk, something I have not yet thought possible that would make things lighter and more beautiful.

A runner's form contains their running past enacted through repetition; it is composed through proprioceptive abilities, muscle memory, the history of the body made through movement and touch, combined with the histories that have been inherited or imposed. Form can be affected by injuries, fitness gains, and steady holding plateaus. Good running form lets you gaze to the horizon. To get there, try to keep your neck and back in alignment, and engage your core. Shoulders should be relaxed. If you get tense, you'll feel them creeping up to your ears; when this happens, shake out your arms, and that should bring them down. Keep your arms moving from heart to side in an even manner, your hands in loose fists, so that you gently punch the air over and over and over again. Let your feet fall directly under your hips. Lean forward a little to let the wind flow past and over you; you don't always have to resist so much.

Form is style too. And in running, as in writing, form has consequences.

On the Subversive Nature of This Handbook

There's an enduring trend across popular running books that connects the practice of running, especially long-distance running, to an ancient or primal art—even to human destiny. These books frame running as something that has been paradoxically lost by the majority of people, despite the ever-growing numbers of recreational runners, marathoners, and ultramarathoners since the 1970s. The authors who take this track insist that the running they've "found" is purer than what you'd see at your local 5K or big-city marathon. This more "authentic" running, which is often done barefoot or in minimal sandals, has been miraculously retained by a few monks, sages, or secluded people living off the grid who have been "discovered" by the authors or their main characters. In this genre of running books, writers or their main characters, and often both, have traveled somewhere, abroad or to the hinterlands of their own country, to extract the "secrets" of authentic running. The authors, then, want to transmit these secrets to readers—

runners and the running-curious—who have picked up their books.

These books get a lot of people running. I admire that they do, but they often do so through fantasies of human universalism or through an exoticizing lens that turns running cultures outside of the author's own into living mythologies. Running books that take this path are also riddled with weird misogyny, strange essentialisms, and casual racism. In these stories, the main characters, who are almost always men, are written as countervailing caricatures who run in opposition to all the ills of the world. In at least one famous running book, which I won't mention by name, the author employs the oldest trick in the book of misogyny—turning all the powerful women he brings into the text into witches. He repeatedly describes how his white male hero calls the champion ultrarunner Ann Trason a *bruja*, a witch, who will be run down like a deer to be slaughtered during a particularly grueling race. Later, in a classic "playing Indian" moment, the writer lingers on a scene where his hero bestows "spirit animal" names onto a group of ultrarunners who have gathered for a race in rural Mexico.[1] In a scene meant to carry meaning and to work as a bonding moment between athletes, the same guy who fantasized about running down Trason gives Jenn Shelton, the next and only other woman ultrarunner who appears in the book, the moniker *la brujita bonita*, the pretty little witch. Meanwhile, most of the men get names like *el oso*, *el coyote*, *el gavilán*, and *el lobo joven*—the bear, coyote, hawk, and young wolf—but the most accomplished US ultrarunner among them, who runs with he/him pronouns, is given the sobriquet *el venado*, the deer, marked as the one to be run down in a misplaced fantasy of persistence hunting transported to Mexico.

I need to put some distance between this approach and style of writing about running and my own. As a white vegetarian from Appalachia, I will not lay claim to an inner "Bushman" with a need for chasing down prey. No matter how many mountain miles I climb, as a non-Buddhist, my ascents and descents will always take on a different spiritual tenor than those of running monks. My running history is not the same as the histories of the Indigenous runners of the Americas, those runners who are framed as "lost," who, to the bewilderment of the white people writing about them, are still out there running, coterminous. I am awed by the many feats of endurance of the Rarámuri who run hundreds of miles at a time through the Copper Canyon in the Chihuahua state of Mexico; amazed by the Tendai Buddhist monks who cover marathon distances over the sacred Mount Hiei in Japan, the most committed doing so for one thousand days in a spiritual practice called *kaihōgyō*, or "circling the mountain"; and impressed by the Xo and Gwi people of the central Kalahari Desert in southern Africa who practice persistence hunting by chasing down steenbok, kudu, and red hartebeest, but these practices and ways of running do not feel like my birthright. Instead I stay delighted by the unique rhythms and practices that emerge whenever and wherever people run, practices that can rhyme and stretch toward each other but still retain their particularities and are never exact copies.

What if humans weren't born to run, and most modern runners just choose to do so because we like it? What if runners run because our practice is encouraged by the cultures we were born into, in similar and different ways to the examples of the running people above? Or, because something else we can't totally explain compels us to do so?

I do not dispute that typical human runners have many affordances that enable us to run well and for long distances: bipedal uprightness that aids in thermoregulation, letting the sun beat down primarily on our heads instead of on our long backs; sweat glands that keep us from overheating; springy Achilles tendons; the ligament on the back of our necks that keeps our heads from bopping around too much; and our powerful butts that help to drive us forward. There are also many runners who run exceptionally well without all of these things, as the expansion of high-tech prostheses throughout the sport of running shows. The most famous and visible of these are carbon fiber blades, like those worn by Paralympians. Still, even with all this useful equipment, possibility is not destiny, and it doesn't explain practice. I think why people run is an open question, where the answer can change with every practice, rather than something that can be pinned down by a hot take or an argument that can settle. Running is a moving thing.

My running finds its origins in the late twentieth century, small-town Tennessee, and my queer American heart. I was inspired by the running handbooks and magazines like *Runner's World* that were around when I first fell in love with running, the "Just Do It" ethos of the era, and the excitement of watching the Olympics in the 1980s and 1990s, when I still thought of America as a superpower. As Roland Barthes writes in *A Lover's Discourse*: "No love is original." It is an "affective contagion," passed like a baton stretching from "others, from the language, from books, from friends," and from popular culture, which he calls "a machine for showing desire."[2] From the familial, social, cultural, and political soup in which I was raised, inchoate desires and identifications around runners and running were stirred within me. Running was in the air of the America I was born into, so much so that when the French philosopher Jean Baudrillard traveled across the country, he declared that running was suicide, adultery, anorexia, and even America itself. He lamented that Americans no longer touch each other, but instead go jogging.[3] Not being a runner himself, Baudrillard missed that running is full of joy, desire, and indulgence in the pleasure and weirdness of having a body, and that running is touching too.

I remember thinking that running was the coolest thing in the world when I watched Florence Griffith-Joyner, better known as Flo-Jo, speed through the eighties in one-legger tights, with her signature long, wavy hair flowing and her bedazzled, colorful nails. She was as futuristic and world-changing for me as David Bowie was for others. Once there was Flo-Jo, the rhythm and composition of track and field would never be the same. She still holds the world record times for the 100 and 200 meters, which she set in 1988. She was also the first Black female athlete from track and field to receive huge endorsements and commercial recognition, doing so well in the market that people called her "Cash-Flo." There was even a Flo-Jo doll released on the Barbie model, kitted out with hot-pink one-legger tights and turquoise briefs with a gold lamé tote bag, hairbrush, and tiny Mizuno "fast track running shoes" as accessories. I want to call this doll an action figure because when I think of Flo-Jo, I always think of her in motion, but I am wary of saying so, of doing anything that might be read as an attempt to masculinize her, the way so many Black women athletes have been denied recognition of their genders.

I also remember the rumors that Carl Lewis was gay, and that although he always asserted otherwise, this speculation and his sometimes gruff and standoffish personality hurt his chances for endorsements and the big money his talent might have gotten him in the American market. Despite his wild success for US track and field, winning nine gold medals and one silver in the Olympics, most of Lewis's lucrative endorsements and commercial opportunities came from Europe and Japan. In overseas arenas, Lewis was relieved to escape the comparisons to Jesse Owens and even Little Richard, based on his flattop haircut, that he received at home. I remember feeling a sting that I couldn't quite name as people traded I-told-you-so's when Lewis appeared in red high-heeled shoes in the advertising campaign for Pirelli tires shot by the photographer Annie Liebowitz in the 1990s. What sticks with me today is how beautiful and strong Lewis looks and how much courage and trust it must have taken to pose for those images.

And I will never forget watching Joan Benoit waving her white cap as she entered the stadium to take her final lap and win the first women's Olympic marathon in 1984 in Los Angeles. I like to think her jaunty gesture, dogged endurance, and androgynous body imprinted possibility in me. Even today when it is dark and cold outside as I start to run, I think of the commercials Benoit made for Nike in the 1980s, the extraordinary ordinariness of even the greatest, tying up her waffle-soled runners, stretching, grabbing a windbreaker, and then logging mile after mile, always in her snowy Maine. In those advertisements meant to sell us shoes, I still find the poetics of practice and a resonant theory of running.

I had no idea until much later that 1984 was the first year women had been allowed to run the marathon in the Olympics, nearly one hundred years after the men; it never occurred to me that men would compete in distances that were felt to be out of reach for women. I'm looking forward to the day when the Olympic marathon will have categories for athletes with genders that do not fit within the current gendered structures of competition, and for when it will not occur to others to think that it was ever any different. Following in the footsteps of Joan Ullyot's handbook *Running Free: A Guide for Women Runners and Their Friends* (1980), this book is "about the changes that running can induce, not only in the individual, but also in old established institutions . . . even perhaps, if we're lucky, the International Olympic Committee!"[4]

Alongside and in between the summer Olympic games, which only come around every four years, I was raised on sports movie training montages. Through the films of my youth, I was socialized to love and fetishize practice nearly as much as winning, maybe more so. I remember the English and Scottish runners dressed in white Henley shirts and shorts to their knees, barefoot on the sand, full of joy, training in the surf, from *Chariots of Fire*. And while the scene of all the lads running on the beach to the asynchronic synth rhythm composed by Vangelis is the more famous, I can never forget the dandyish way the British hurdler Andrew Lindsay whips off his scarf, gives two quick shakes of his arms, and then sets off elegantly leaping, trying not to spill the champagne filling the coupe glasses that rest on each obstacle. He knocks the last hurdle a bit, and the camera zooms in to catch the slight sloshing, which only adds to the pleasure of the practice scene.

And I remember Sylvester Stallone in *Rocky IV* wearing a bomber jacket to train in Siberia, the land of his nemesis. Rocky was doing things old-school, pulling sleds like an overgrown husky, clomping through half-frozen streams, and muscling through knee-high snow carrying a huge log on his shoulders. The montage flips back and forth between Rocky and the ice-blond Soviet powerhouse Ivan Drago, who was simultaneously training, but with punching drills punctuated by steroid injections in a high-tech, doctor-laden laboratory atmosphere. In the scenes with Ivan, his wife, Ludmilla, a former Soviet Olympic swimmer, is always there as a visual cue of the mysterious cold beauty of our rivals. The juxtaposition of Rocky and Ivan hit home the not-so-subtle superpower versus superpower subtext, showing Americans as hardworking good guys and the Soviets as robotic, heartless cheaters.

Montages like these still stick with me even when final cinematic knockout scenes and Olympic podium denouements can no longer be recalled. The rhythm of a typical sports movie montage lights up a pleasure center laid down in my memory, and I would live inside this cadence if I could. The predictable cycle goes like this: an athlete overcomes multiple setbacks; slowly their body bends to and with the monotony, agony, and ecstasy of practice; and then all that practice gathers up and we can see everything come together, and just when the athlete

needs it to! Montages are a surefire method to open me up to imaginations of possibility through practice.

My earliest ideas about running were also shaped by the running handbooks and ephemera that existed in my childhood home, especially James Fixx's *The Complete Book of Running*. I remember taking it down from the bookshelf in our wood-paneled living room and spending time trying to learn how to create a running life like the one the book promised. The cover was Coca-Cola red with a pair of lean-muscled runner's legs in motion; a hint of red split-side shorts peeked out from under the title. The feet were graced with red nylon Onitsuka Tiger racing flats with the iconic white logo designed to symbolize a tiger's tail. I was fascinated by those shoes, those legs. And I wasn't the only one; the author's legs in running shoes became a national fetish. Fixx had worn those red shoes in the 1978 Boston Marathon, and although I didn't know it at the time, they were also a sign that he was a serious runner. Racing flats were still pretty rare in those days, and you often had to make an effort to track some down by going to a specialty running store, ordering them by mail, or buying a pair out of the trunk of someone's car at a race. If you knew enough to pick up on it, you'd know this book was for marathon racers, as well as for beginners. And if you were a novice, or running-curious, you could still appreciate the strength and style on display.

The iconic cover image was shot by the New York photographer Neal Slavin in his SoHo apartment utilizing a makeshift track for the background. The publisher, Random House, didn't like the image. They didn't think a book with a man's legs on the cover would sell, but ultimately because of a time crunch for publication they went with it anyway.[5] After all, it was only a handbook about running—who would want to read such a thing? It turned out that quite a lot of people did. *The Complete Book of Running* was number one on the *New York Times* best-seller list for weeks. It went on to sell over a million copies. Odds are if you were alive during the 1970s or 1980s in the United States, and you, your parents, or whoever you lived with even thought about running, there was a copy of Fixx's handbook lying around your house too.

I returned to Fixx while writing my own handbook to revisit the running world I was born into. The opening section is titled "On the Subversive Nature of This Book," wherein he promises "first to introduce you to the extraordinary world of running and second to change your life."[6] This is a bold start. Although Fixx's enthusiasm is contagious and his writing can make thoughts of personal bests dance in your head, the real subversion of this handbook comes from the writer's own at times raw display of his love for running and his need to write it all down, to convey a runner's lifestyle, as he sees it. I'm sure I didn't understand this as a child when I leafed through the pages. I don't fully understand it now.

I can place the "whens" of my running, the beginning, and the ebbs and flows of injury and energy, the increases and decreases of mileage, but the "whys" and the ongoingness are much more difficult to convey. When people ask me why I run, I can string a few sentences together, but they always feel inadequate. I often use one or a combination of these responses: "to see if I can go the distance," "to qualify for the Boston Marathon," "to balance my neurosis," "to think . . . rumor has it that Alan Turing created the computer on a run," "I'm just a person who needs to exhaust myself." These things do feel true, but they also feel inadequate. Running, like most practices and attractions approached with fervor, is notoriously difficult to understand and explain. It needs a bit of space and time to spool out, to compose a story that is always on the move.

I can't know exactly where my love for running and my desire to keep running come from. I don't know if they were imprinted in me as a child when I was just learning what my body could do or if they took root after years of practice carved a groove in me and now it just feels right. And maybe part of the subversive nature of this handbook is to show that runners weren't necessarily born this way, and that the point is not to show a primal source for our desire to run but to see what we can invent and learn from the practice as we go along. Some of us might have chosen running because it seemed like a good option among all the myriad ways to spend time, and some of us might have been drawn to it for as long as we can remember. Some might choose today to go on a run, their first or thousandth, and by that very action become or continue to be a runner.

In *The Complete Book of Running*, Fixx writes, "If you miss the pleasure of running you miss its essence."[7] Fair warning: this small handbook does not aim for completion and will not even try to explain the essential heart of running. I do not believe such an essence exists, but that each runner's heart brings what Michel Foucault calls new "affective intensities" to the practice, "which at one and the same time keep it going and shake it up."[8] Foucault is not writing about running, but his thinking on love, queer desire, and relationality has colored my thinking about modes of living in general, including running.

By thinking about what and who running touches, I am able to hook together paragraphs that show some ways that running moves people through distance, time, races, accidents, and patterns of practice that lightly link together through loops of repetition. While I try to outrun essentialism to keep things open, I do want to keep pleasure as a running partner, and one thing I know for sure is that to get to pleasure you have to go through practice.

A Note on "Just Do It"

Nike's simple slogan—half taunt, half order—seemed to be as much about sex or drugs as about running or sporting. Introduced in 1988, it sounded like a counterargument to Nancy Reagan's Just Say No campaign from the War on Drugs and the teenage abstinence initiatives of the era. "Just Do It" was quintessentially American in its casualness and its veneer of daring. And like much of American culture, the inspiration for Nike's ad campaign has a dark backstory. It comes from the double murderer Gary Gilmore, who robbed and killed a gas station attendant and then a motel worker in Utah in 1976. Gilmore weighed heavily on the public imagination not only for the murders he committed but also because he asked for the death penalty.[1] When given the opportunity to share any last words before he was to be executed by a firing squad, Gilmore said: "Let's do it." This simple phrase inspired Dan Weiden from the ad agency Weiden + Kennedy as he developed the "Just Do It" ad campaign for Nike.[2] With Nike, the collective contraction

"let's" falls back into history, and the pressure of American individualism is set in the recognizable Futura Bold Condensed font.[3] Nike's "Just Do It," a phrase twisted from a murderer's last words, cast a spell of secular magic and became forever part of the cultural poetics of running. Swoosh goes history.[4]

Leaving It All on the Track

**Eighth-Grade Mile Relay, Conference Championship,
Morristown, Tennessee, 1992**

When the aluminum baton hit my palm, the runner in the lead had already loped around the first curve. As anchor, last leg, it would be up to me: I set off, manic and determined. I was frenetic will on two skinny legs sticking out of nylon shorts hurling myself around the red oval marked with clean white lines. My opponent seemed to be running a different race entirely; her stride was easy and confident, the posture of a victory ensured. By going flat out, I managed to catch up to her with half a lap to go. When she heard me closing in, her head swiveled around and her eyes registered surprise. This gave me a rush of energy, as it always does when I read on someone's face that they've underestimated me.

A new race was on. With my approach the front-runner shifted into another gear. She tried a surge to lose me. I hung on. I tried a surge, and she matched me. I moved into the second lane, "the Lane of High Hopes," so that I could run alongside her.[1] We picked up the pace together; we were in sync stride for stride, sharing the lead. If we had tied our two inner legs together, we would have made an unbeatable three-legged racing team. But this beautiful moment didn't last. It couldn't. We wanted to crush each other.

Rounding the third turn, I started to fade, my form quickly unraveling, my arms going wild, pummeling the air to try to make up for legs that wouldn't go any faster. Into the final stretch, things devolved further. I tripped a couple of times but somehow managed to stay upright, although wobbly. My vision was going too: I remember the world shifting into monochrome—the green singlet of my opponent fading to gray, the red of the track dulled and taken out from underneath me, the whole world in shadow.

In the last hundred meters, my opponent started to pull away, but there was nothing I could do except try to keep going, even as I felt my body was coming apart at the seams. Just before the finish line my feet tangled again, and I collapsed in a heap across the line: annihilated. I finished in second place, the same place we would have gotten if I had run a controlled race at my normal pace. My coach and teammates came to gather me. They set me down on the grass, and as I lay there motionless, I listened to the voice of Coach Skeen floating above me, her words sounding like a eulogy. I felt a strange happiness in my spectacular failure, more joyful even than when I won the mile, setting the school record, earlier that afternoon.[2]

I had wanted to come from behind to win like Eric Liddell in *Chariots of Fire*, after the French runner pushed him off the track and he picked himself up quickly to sprint to victory. I had always dreamed of hearing something like what he heard while lying in the infield, his heart still racing, as the coach picked him up, saying, "That wasn't the prettiest quarter I've ever seen . . . but certainly the bravest," and I did. The happiness came from going all out, as the expression "left it all on the track" indicates. But what was the "it" I had left? Everything I had, every ounce of energy, but more than that too. The "it," to me, is a diffuseness of all you have to offer, something like personality, something like love. The "it" you can leave on a track is hard to show in other realms of life; this kind of raw exhibition of desire would look erratic in a classroom when you are trying to get an idea across to students or would come off as a too-muchness while having coffee with a person you want badly to turn into a friend. In most areas of life, you can't show how much you want or love things, but in running, and especially in racing, there is the opportunity for this kind of near-naked display. This showcase of desire, effort, and personality is made all the more vulnerable for the fact that, in racing, you are often not wearing much clothing.

The thing about the "it" you leave all of on the track is that it doesn't stay there. It's laid out on the oval only for a moment, and then, like a collapsed runner, it gets picked up by those moved by the performance. It follows you and becomes part of your story and the stories others tell about you. Once left, "it" has an ongoingness.[3] All runners have a few races like my middle school mile relay final, races that they feel define them as a runner and by extension clarify them as a person, both to themselves and to others. It wasn't a good idea to run in the second lane, which meant that I was running a slightly longer distance than my opponent, and it wasn't smart to set out at a full sprint. If I had been faster or run a better race, made ground more slowly, slotted myself behind the front-runner in the first lane and let her take the drag of the wind, and then chosen one moment to pass and kick, we might have won, but I had no mind for strategy then. And even now, although I dream of a controlled elegance, if I'm honest, my default mode takes the shape of ragged will.

Thirty years later I can still feel this race, the wild pain of pushing my body to collapse and the warm presence of the other runner on my left, wanting the same thing I wanted: to finish, to win, to move those watching, to make contact with each other, with ourselves and the world, to touch and be touched. How do I know this runner felt something akin to what I did? I know from running beside her, by her affirmative answer to every question I asked with my body: Can you do this? Can you hold on? Will you bury me?

Running Is a Contact Sport

Inaugural London Marathon, 1981

I know who to look for because I've watched a video of this race dozens of times: the Minnesotan Dick Beardsley in the New Balance kit with a light gray top and black shorts, wearing shoes with the flame-red *N*, who leads from the beginning, and the slightly taller Norwegian Inge Simonsen in a black-and-white Nike singlet sporting blue shoes with a white Swoosh. If you haven't watched this race before or learned its outcome, you couldn't know that Simonsen is the one to fix your attention on from the small pack of runners who stay right behind Beardsley for over half of the race. You would figure this out as the course winds around the Isle of Dogs, where Beardsley kicks up the pace by running a very fast mile, and Simonsen is the only one of the pack to answer. In the BBC video I rewatch, a reporter comments as the two runners speed away: "Well, there's a Norwegian and an American and they look set for a head-to-head

confrontation. This is what the marathon is all about. They've run sixteen miles; they've got another ten miles to go. And we now know who's fit enough, let's find out who's brave enough."[1]

Over the next nine miles, Beardsley is pushing the pace more often, but they are both trying to wear each other out. In the last mile, Simonsen pulls up next to Beardsley, and for the first time they are running parallel. It looks like it could be either marathoner's race. Then, with about a quarter of a mile to go, Simonsen says something to Beardsley. They run a bit more, and Beardsley says something back to him. The BBC reporter wonders aloud if they are planning to come in together. He speculates that Simonsen might not speak very much English, but that "as an experienced runner, he'd have gotten the message. Do they battle it out or do they come in together?" This is a risky question to hang in the air of the last stage of a marathon, especially without a shared language.

The answer seems to come in a beautiful synchroneity of matching strides. The two runners do not appear to be making any effort to outrace each other even as the clock ticking above the finish line comes into sight, but anything could happen in these last moments; "a yes can always shift to the no, stretch itself" into its opposite.[2] Trust is a fragile thing in competition. In the final moments, Simonsen reaches for Beardsley, misses, reaches again, and this time catches hold of him. They run a few paces hand in hand, then raise their arms in elation, breaking the tape together in a dead heat at 2:11:48. As the tape unfurls, the word *London* briefly meets Simonsen's forearm and *Gillette* frames his ribs, while *Marathon* slides across Beardsley's torso. The two exhausted marathoners take a couple of lumbering steps with their arms around each other in a seesawing side hug. Then Simonsen ruffles Beardsley's hair. As I watch this gesture, the corporate sponsor's jingle "Gillette, the best a man can get" sings in my head, and for once it feels true. We've found out who's fit enough and who's brave enough.

In the postrace interview with the BBC, Beardsley, rosy-cheeked and mustachioed, full of joy, is impossible not to like. He says: "I feel great. I feel very good. A super day to run a race, you couldn't find better conditions, a super course. . . . The Norwegian, we uh, broke away from the other guys at about sixteen miles, then it was just a duking out between me and him; he'd put in a surge and I'd put in a surge trying to break each other, then with about a half mile to go we just kind of looked at each other and gave a wink." I love how Beardsley doesn't know or can't remember Simonsen's name in the moment. The race becomes an encounter, where what matters is created through the chase, the effort, the vulnerability, and shared desire. Who these guys are to one another emerges through the space of the marathon.

The moment when the runners' hands meet reminds me of a passage in James Fixx's *Complete Book of Running*, where he writes: "I know of no closer feeling between two athletes than to be running stride for stride in the twenty-fifth mile of a grueling marathon. Both know that one will cross the finish line first, and will thus, for the record book, win, but each knows that his own fatigue and pain are indistinguishable from the other's. This shared experience draws them together far more strongly than their competitiveness drives them apart."[3] Like Fixx, I couldn't have imagined the possibility of a hand-in-hand tie before I saw one, and certainly not one decided together on the fly. And what's more, I wouldn't have imagined that I would be moved by such an ending. I was molded by a win-at-all-costs-or-lose-spectacularly-trying American sporting culture. I usually find ties anticlimactic and disappointing. But watching these two runners holding hands across the finish line does something to me; it surprises me, by gentling my assumptions about what competition can be and by giving shape to an aesthetic vision beyond success and failure. The beauty of this race, for me, is that it catches me off guard, as I catch the runners catching themselves being unguarded. They are vulnerable to each other, and they know it. They have maxed out their efforts, and they know it. They are aware of this individually, and they understand that it is the same for the other; they know by running beside each other that they want the same thing; they know that they can give it to each other, and so they do.

I've watched this marathon over and over while writing this handbook because I've been thinking about how, what, and who running touches. With Beardsley and Simonsen, I see in running what the writer Joyce Carol Oates sees in boxing, "part dance, courtship and coupling."[4] As the two runners break away from the pack, they test each other, tease, make passes, wink, hold hands, and embrace. They touch each other, and this touch extends out, it stretches through time and space—touching the cheering crowd lining the streets of London in the rain, those taking in the BBC live in 1981, and me, watching them race again and again, forty years later on my laptop. I rewatch this race to be touched by a gesture that is already a poem, to touch something beautiful about running and what running can do, and to see something I didn't know was possible until I saw it.

Running after Olympians

I joined my college track team on a lark. I was out for a run around campus when some runners I knew shouted at me from their practice session: "Hey, Lindsey, run with us!" I waved them off, thinking they were teasing me. Then someone said: "Come on, get over here." And so I did. I practiced with the team that day, the next, and the one following. I kept showing up at the encouragement of my friends, and no one seemed to mind, including the coach. At the end of the week, he asked me to his office and invited me to join the team officially with a small scholarship. I said yes easily. This gives you a sense of the kind of ad hoc track-and-field operation Wofford College was running back in the late 1990s.

Even though I had not raced on a track competitively since middle school, I ran regularly, and I played soccer, a game filled with running. I felt I could do it. Another reason to join track was to travel with the team, to go to meets, to get away. I was unhappy at college. Wofford was a tiny, conservative southern school located in the small town of Spartanburg, South Carolina, a place so lacking in charm that it was ironically called "Sparkle City." The school's motto, "There's a right way, a wrong way, and a Wofford way," could have given me a clue to the insularity and stubborn adherence to the kind of imaginations of a good life I would find there, but the phrase was just vague enough to mean almost anything. I was drawn to Wofford by the chance to play NCAA Division I soccer, which was my primary sport, but I had offers from other schools. My decision fell largely to which coach called me first, and the call happened to come from Spartanburg. Other coaches telephoned soon after, but I felt that I had already committed and turned down all my other options. This is a choice I've often regretted.

At eighteen, I had little understanding of the world and the spaces where I might move most freely and joyfully. I had not yet learned that "in college you substitute enthusiasm for love," as Kathleen Stewart and Lauren Berlant write.[1] Before I arrived, college had seemed like a magical ticket to ideas, friendship, and adult life. I thought I would be able to find my pack of punks and weirdos anywhere, and I did, but the conservative atmosphere of the place, driven by Old South gendered expectations, the predominance of fraternities and sororities, racism, and homophobia, took its toll. I was looking for a kind of freedom that was not easy to find there. It was a lonely time. I drank a lot (soccer girls like to party), developed an ulcer, and dreamed of transferring but felt too depressed to make any steps to do so. One after another, I watched good friends leave for other schools but couldn't follow their lead. It didn't help that I was figuring out I was queer in a space where no one was out and where it didn't feel safe to be so. This is hard to imagine today when so many professional soccer players on women's teams are celebrated for their queerness, but it was a different world for me then.

It would take until 2013 for the US women's national team striker Abby Wambach to announce her gayness to the public. Twenty years to hear US soccer star Megan Rapinoe exclaim: "You can't win a championship without gays on your team—it's never been done before, ever. That's science, right there!"[2] The same twenty years to see Rapinoe's teammate Kelley O'Hara kiss her girlfriend in the stands with no explanation necessary after winning the 2019 World Cup.

At Wofford, things were better for me during soccer season, when my days were organized around the rhythm of classes, studying, practice, and games, but when it ended or I was side-lined by injury, a malaise seeped in. The off-season took on a double meaning; it not only meant a break from running with a pack, scoring and assisting goals, the highs and lows of winning and losing, the disappointment or resignation to ties; it also described my emotional state, the sliding into a sad, flat zone. During these off-times I felt best when I was running. I organized my schedule to give me as much time as possible to leave campus for the soft pine-needled paths in the Piedmont area of South Carolina and the mountain laurel, sourwood, and tulip poplar–laden trails through the Blue Ridge Mountains of North Carolina. On days filled with classes, I would run around dingy Spartanburg and discover things that delighted me, things that I could see only when I was moving.

In the winter of my sophomore year, I got up before dawn every day to run with my friend Kate. When she landed at Wofford, she felt, as I had, like she was from another world. Neither of us had understood the multilayeredness of the American South; we had both wrongly assumed that a small liberal arts college in South Carolina would feel similar to the Florida coast where Kate was from or to the Appalachian towns where I grew up. When we ran together, I could sometimes close the distance between what I felt and what I thought I would feel when I arrived in Spartanburg. The trick was to get going before anything could hold us back. We'd meet when the sky was still navy in front of her dorm, and then do some loops around the sleepy town. All our loops had names. The one I remember now had us going around our favorite pizza place: the Venus Pie loop. Our paces were a good match, and running with Kate had a formal pleasure to it, along with a feeling of camaraderie I so badly needed. We always walked or ran as slowly as we could muster over the speed bumps, pretending that we were moving so fast we'd need to slow down to adhere to the law. These runs were almost always the best part of my day, when I felt the most ease in myself, and the most joy. Running took the edge off the off-season, it dulled the throb of loneliness and slowed the grind of disappointment.

When the invitation came to join the track team in the spring of my sophomore year, I imagined myself on weekends on other campuses warming up on green, grassy infields, running around symmetrical ovals, sitting in brightly colored bleachers with Kate and other track-and-field friends, still closeted, but also freed by the regimented rhythms of track life. Plus, I have always loved watching track and field. I am drawn to sports where you can see athletes' bodies in motion, where practitioners are not hidden behind helmets and bulky uniforms, and where you can see the drama playing out not only in facial expressions but also through limbs, tensed and springy. As the Scottish indie pop band Belle and Sebastian sing in "The Stars of Track and Field," athletes are "beautiful people."[3] I wanted to be close to these beautiful people, and to be one too.

Stuart Murdoch, the lead singer of Belle and Sebastian, had been a serious runner before a three-year bout with myalgic encephalomyelitis, a type of chronic fatigue syndrome, even running the Glasgow Marathon in 1986 in a very fast 2:57:08 when he was only seventeen. He wrote the lyrics to "The Stars of Track and Field" during his illness when he was homebound at his parents' house, fantasizing about his desire to run and to inhabit his body again like an athlete. The song is dreamy and full of the kind of longing that creates a world where a nerdy runner can stretch toward something beautiful and in doing so become more beautiful themselves. Since I first heard it, the song has been a mixtape staple, and as I reflect on it now while writing this handbook, I realize that it is part of my theory of what running is and can do. "The Stars of Track and Field" is an anthem of those who do not quite fit in, of the lonely and the also-rans. While it seems to celebrate the winners, it is the interiority of the dreamers, those longing to touch and be touched by the sporting atmosphere and their fellow athletes, that is given voice.

My soccer coach did not want me to run the longest distances, so as not to lose the fast-twitch muscles needed for the quick sprints that game demands. So I ran the 800 meters and the half mile, although I was much more suited to the 1,500 meters, 5,000 meters, or better yet, the 10,000 meters.

Some distances have an aura that lends runners prestige in the popular imagination. The 100 meters makes a runner almost a superhero, the fastest person in the world! (or at least on the track in any given meet). It doesn't hurt when the runner has a name like the Jamaican sprinter Usain Bolt! The mile has a classic, even aristocratic, allure, driven in part by the celebration of the British runner Roger Bannister breaking the four-minute mile in 1954 at the Iffley Road track at Oxford University. The sub-four-minute mile was imagined for a very long time to be a barrier of human performance, much like the sub-two-hour marathon in competition is today, although that barrier too seems likely to go any time now. The Kenyan runner Eliud Kipchoge ran a 1:59:40 marathon in a closed-course trial in 2019, so it is likely that he or someone else will get under the two-hour mark very soon.[4]

While the marathon garners respect for the endurance it takes, it also retains a romantic and mythological hold thanks in part to the story of an ancient Greek foot messenger sent to deliver news of victory over the Persians from the city of Marathon to Athens. Robert Browning popularized the myth in his poem "Pheidippides" (1879), drawing on ancient histories from Herodotus, Lucian, and Plutarch while employing poetic license. In Browning's poem, Pheidippides runs swiftly for about twenty-five miles, delivers the news—"Rejoice!"—and then drops dead from exhaustion.[5] Browning's poetics hang over the modern marathon; to finish one is to rejoice and die a little, only to live and run again.

To the uninitiated the 800 meters, by contrast, is the Wednesday of track events; no ancient mythical gloss graces it, no fantasy of superhuman transcendence rests on its two laps. From the outside it can be seen as a middle distance to simply get through, and because it is not often marked to be anything special, it can slip by unnoticed and unremarked upon. To be inside the 800 in motion is another matter altogether. It is a mad hazard without the swagger of sprints or the pleasures of going long. The half mile is a gut race, brutal both psychologically and physically: too short to make up a lot of ground if you go through a bad spot, and too long to purely muscle through. Make any wrong move and you will be severely punished.

Like most runners, I am guilty of fetishizing the particular kinds of suffering our sport produces and then micro-fetishizing down to particular races and distances. The magic of training for a run of a particular length is that you can find camaraderie through time and space with others who have suffered in similar and adjacent ways; it puts you in a long-distance relationship with those who share your event, no matter the distance. Through my half-mile racing experiences, I can stretch a thread of connection to Otto Peltzer, a gay, antifascist German runner from the 1920s, known by his nicknames "Otto the Strange" and "The Stork." I can keep this thread going to the contemporary queer South African runner Caster Semenya, who for so many years, as she beat her competitors, was hounded by officials, track bureaucrats, and jealous runners who cried and continue to cry that her body is unfair, that she is too muscular, has too much testosterone, that she is too strong and too fast—too good. This winding thread reaches also to Nikki Hiltz, one of the first out nonbinary runners in the professional ranks, who runs with they/them pronouns in women's events. I can feel some kind of kinship through running—through distance—despite our various gendered, racialized, historical, social, political, and cultural contexts, and the vast gap in quality between those professional runners and myself. I know that all of us half-milers have felt those two laps exercising us, that we have a shared experience of the play of speed on our bodies, imprinting us with distance in time.

My primary goal when running college track was to prove to myself that I belonged there by not coming in last. Wofford was the smallest college in NCAA Division I athletics, which is part of why our mascot was a terrier. We ran against huge universities with world-class athletes. I never got the feeling that our coach expected any of us to win a race. Living up to that expectation, I never placed first, but I never came in dead last either. Each race, I would head to the line in my warm-up sweats or, if it was hot, long soccer shorts, waiting for the absolute last moment to peel them off. I was shy about my body in those days, which I attribute to a general dysphoria that I have never experienced before or since. Standing around in my racing briefs and singlet, I felt vulnerable, which is not what you want before a race. When I was racing, the self-consciousness of my body took a different shape and tenor. I thought mostly of form, and how I could hold it at pace. My strategy was to try to stay with the lead pack in the first lap, act like I could run

there, and then hang on as closely as I could for the second and final lap. It was a reckless approach, but not an uncommon one for half-milers; many of us go in for what is called in running parlance "positive splits," meaning the first half is run faster than the second. If the second half is run faster, then you've run a negative split.

I never ran as fast in practice as in a race. I needed the context, and the other runners, to help me find another gear. Racing is voluntarily entering into the unknown. You practice and train, which might give you a sense of what you can do, but on any given day you could surprise yourself. When you are racing you can sometimes have the feeling, as the poet and runner Devin Kelly writes, "of being as far along the edge of yourself as possible."[6] Sometimes I even sensed that I crossed this threshold, that I was running beyond myself, and having been touched by the tang of speed, I was taken up by the rhythms of the pack and carried along outside my control. Although it didn't show from the outside, many times, and this is embarrassing to say because it is a short race, I felt that I might not be able to finish the second lap, that I would come completely undone. I even had this uncertain feeling when I set my college record at a meet at Coastal Carolina University, when afterward my coach told me I had run a time worthy of a "real runner." I wondered what category I had been racing under up until that point.

Every time I crossed the finish line, I experienced relief and an I-pulled-it-off wash of pleasure. I felt a similar feeling after classes in the first semesters when I started teaching undergraduates; I still feel it sometimes. There were other pleasures to track too. I delighted in learning speed drills like fartleks,

Virén sprints, and striders. I relished tightening up my racing spikes with a spike key, as if my shoes were wind-up toys getting ready to do their thing like some nineteenth-century automatons. I adored the warm-up suits with those satisfying front zippers that end in a rectangular mock turtleneck just below the chin. I loved the concussion of colors that track meets bring. I love tracks. Just looking at their clean oval shape makes my spine feel good and lights up my haptic sense. This is maybe why I've never cottoned to the short races as much; on a track, I want to see runners go around at least once; I want to see them handle the curves. This is not to say I haven't adored some of the personalities who took on shorter races—Flo-Jo especially!—but the races themselves always leave me wanting more time with the runners.

When I wrote that I never came in last in one of my college races, I should clarify that I never lost in my own race: the 800 meters. There was one meet at the University of South Carolina when the bus carrying our sprinters had broken down and it was clear they wouldn't make it in time for their races. In a track meet, each team must compete in a certain number of events or face disqualification. When the sprinters didn't show up, the quick races had to be run by the rest of us—field athletes and longer-distance runners. I was recruited to run the 4 × 400 meters relay along with teammates who ran the 1,500 meters and 3,000 meters, and my running partner Kate, who threw the discus. I'll never forget taking off my long shorts to stand at the line next to the runners from South Carolina, the maroon of their uniforms accented with their mascot, the fighting cock, and three of the four relay members with the Olympic rings tattooed right below their racing briefs. Shaking out my scrawny legs, next to these beautifully muscled racers, I have never felt more out of place, less up to the task at hand, and giddier to be somewhere at the same time.

My relay team was quickly left in the dust: the first and second runners had already put us in last place, and a distant last at that. Kate ran third leg and, desperate to stop, tried to hand me the baton too early—her tanned arm with its discus-slinging muscles reaching out is etched in my memory, along with the pleading look on her face, and her soft voice made a little raw from effort saying "stick"— but I couldn't reach. She was too far back, and she had to take two more strides and try again. When the baton finally hit my hand, I was there on the red track running alone, as the Olympians, and those who could compete with Olympians, had long finished. It didn't matter at all what I did, as long as I crossed the line, but I gave my best effort just to see what I could do. Among the Olympic runners I ran against that day were Miki Barber, who ran in the 4 × 400 meters relay for the United States in 2000; Charmaine Howell, who won a silver medal for Jamaica in the 4 × 400 meters relay in 2000; and Tonique Williams-Darling, who competed for the Bahamas in the 400 meters in both the 2000 and the 2004 Olympics, winning the gold medal in 2004. What a joy sometimes to be so completely out of your league and to know you have nothing to lose.

One thing I loved about running track was that it put me in spaces more like those I had grown up in, where I had Black friends and teammates, spaces that were different from many of the all-white social structures I found at Wofford. I am ashamed to say that I only realized after revisiting this race decades later that our team buses had been mostly segregated. There is a larger story here, too, of the soft and not-so-soft segregation of university track-and-field events in the United States, where even today, the majority of sprinters are Black, and the majority of long-distance runners are white.

Running track took me by surprise. It lifted me from a situation in which I felt stuck and gave me a chance to do something I didn't know I was capable of, modest as my track accomplishments were. Running made me glad I stuck around Spartanburg. Joan Didion writes in her essay "On Keeping a Notebook" that if we lose touch with the people we used to be, they "turn up unannounced and surprise us, come hammering on the mind's door at 4 a.m. of a bad night and demand to know who deserted them, who betrayed them, who is going to make amends." Reflecting on college track has always brought me back to my younger self; the thread of distance reaches there too. But only in writing about it did I hit the mood and feel anew the difficult feelings in which I was then mired. Only in writing did I make amends to my younger self for not being able to leave a situation where I felt stuck and lonely.

I still have my Wofford racing singlet, black and white with gold lettering, a bit faded with effort and time. I wore it when I ran my fastest marathon, and I still wear it sometimes when I practice. I ran in it today to see what it would feel like. I imagined it to be like dipping into an old notebook, doing something like research for the handbook. The feeling was similar to writing about my track experience, like running both with and out of my younger self. Didion insists that we should remain on "nodding terms with the people we used to be." Whenever I run, I give younger Lindsey a runner's nod of recognition, and when I run in my Wofford singlet, I touch my younger self, and I know I've run out of something by running through it. This should not be taken as a hero narrative; it is simply a story of everyday endurance, of not being completely ground down by institutions and milieus designed to prevent queer flourishing. Didion writes: "Perhaps it is difficult to see the value in having one's self back in that kind of mood, but I do see it."[7] And I do, too; to begin to tell a story of being stuck or of regret differently is like replacing a busted track spike with a fresh one. You have to find a new point that will grip the curves, like attending to something in the narrative that you only just noticed was wonky, a part that didn't quite track, and taking up your tools, you turn it a little, and then test it to see if you can run on it.

Running Is Your Life

There is a type of interval training done on a track where you jog or float the bends and give a faster, harder effort on the straights. I learned these as "Virén sprints" from my college track coach. The drill is named for the long-distance runner Lasse Virén, who was part of a generation of great Finnish runners in the 1970s known as the "Flying Finns."[1] Virén was famous for incorporating lots of track intervals into his training. My coach had an old VHS tape of a Virén documentary that he lent me called *Running Is Your Life*. I remember sliding it into the little open mouth of the VHS player that was built into the TV I had in my dorm room. The documentary was an introduction to the intense world of Virén's training, and it was mesmerizing.

I remember watching Virén running down an open stretch of a snowy road with a robotic voice-over stating: "You are so hopelessly alone." And I remember him before a competition warming up on the track, with the voice saying: "Getting nervous doesn't help anything, so Lasse doesn't get nervous." I watched this video over and over with some track friends, and we took up these catchphrases to delight each other throughout the season. If we were running in a pack at practice and one of us got too far ahead, we would shout out: "Sara, you are so hopelessly alone." Or if we were trying to psych each other up before a race, we would hold each other by the shoulders and say with put-on seriousness: "Getting nervous doesn't help anything, so Hazel doesn't get nervous."

As I was writing this handbook, I searched online for Lasse Virén and was delighted and surprised that this documentary is available on YouTube. As I rewatched *Running Is Your Life*, it was like sharing a joke with my former self and stretching in memory to the friends I used to run with. I had forgotten the emphasis on friendship that film espouses, which comes as a balm to the loneliness of the long-distance runner we see in the early part of the documentary. Toward the end of the film, the voice asks: "Besides the challenge, can it be that friendship brought them here? All runners experience hard work, discipline, pain, agony, anticipation, glory, a common thread of understanding, respect, and friendship." I take the vague spatial reference "here" to be the space of running, where, as the voice says, "Nothing, yet everything, is important."

As the camera follows Virén's long-legged frame on a training run set to the music of Chopin to close the film, the voice leaves with a direct address: "Many times, you have been asked, when does all this end? Now you know, not for a long, long, time. Running is your life." So go harder on the straights and take it easy on the bends. Repeat until you've had enough, then go hang out with your friends.

Speed Play

Not all speed training needs to be done on the track. While the oval has its pleasures, the forest can be a great place to work on your speed as well. I'm partial to fartleks, which is Swedish for "speed play." In this type of practice, you introduce speed for as long as you feel like it, then slow down but keep running, never stopping, over and over again, until you decide that you're done (or hit the total time or distance you've promised yourself you'd do before you set out). To add some structure to your fartlek workout, you can follow your inner clock for each burst of speed, or you can use cues in the landscape, by racing to a specific tree or up a particular hill, for example. The practice is often traced back to the Swedish coach Gösta Holmér, who in the 1940s had his runners do interval training in nature, rather than on the track, and by changing their speed and rhythm on the fly. The Swedes would run like this for miles and miles on soft pine-needled forest paths, making them some of the best distance runners in the world at that time. Don't worry, though.

Even if you don't have access to forests, you can still fartlek almost anywhere. Sometimes I like to do this kind of workout by color. If I'm running in a city or in a busy park, I'll start running hard when I see someone in pink, for example, and allow myself to back off when I see someone in yellow. If you start to feel that your running is a grind or simply a means to an end, more like what boxers call "roadwork" than an opening into joy or catharsis, speed play can be an antidote. You can fartlek alone or with others. Follow your heart.

Personal Best

The film *Personal Best* was released in 1982 between *Chariots of Fire* and *Rocky IV*, but unlike those sports films that floated predominantly in the popular culture in my youth, I didn't encounter it until years later. It wasn't suggested to me by my lesbian boss at Blockbuster Video, who was constantly sending me home with movies like *Bound*, *High Art*, and *Chasing Amy*—the last film a particular object of fascination because of its general terribleness and the fact that Ben Affleck's character was a dead ringer for my college track coach. I didn't find out about *Personal Best*, like many people in my friend circle, through Ellen DeGeneres's 1997 coming-out episode on her self-named sitcom. In that episode Ellen says to her therapist, played by Oprah Winfrey: "Oh, why did I ever rent *Personal Best*?!" And her therapist responds that she can't put *this* on the media. Then the laugh track does its thing.

While I would have watched any movie framed, even jokingly, as powerful enough to make someone gay, I found my way to Robert Towne's film about a lesbian love affair between two track-and-field athletes through jangly guitar and earnest lyrics, when I brought home the album *Personal Best* by the feminist queercore punk band Team Dresch, named in homage to the film. Queer music scenes have often been my best education.

There's a lot not to like about Towne's film: the missed opportunity to talk about the Cold War, the compulsory heterosexuality, casual anti-Asian and anti-Indigenous racism, out-of-the-blue antiqueerness, and weird misogyny. But what the film does get right is the formlessness of queer friendship and the hapticality of runners. The film is bookended by the Olympic Trials of 1976 and 1980, and the action swirls around the relationship between Chris Cahill, played by a young Mariel Hemingway, and Tory Skinner, played by Pat Donnelly, a real-life Olympic hurdler who at one time was ranked fourth in the world. Throughout the film, the runners fall into the rhythm of a relationship, train together, break up, and compete against each another in the pentathlon.

The pentathlon is a combined track-and-field event composed of five disciplines held in one day in this order: 100-meter hurdles, high jump, shot put, long jump, and the 800 meters.[1] Hemingway trained for a year in order to perform all these events convincingly. She was particularly nervous about the hurdling. In the film, she plays an up-and-coming track star, and she looks like an athlete. Then you see her running along the beach with her lesbian love interest and teammate, and you can spy the difference. Donnelly's running is smoother and lighter with the ease that comes with years of running at a high level. I love these moments when the film inadvertently captures how practice gathers behind unseen, perceptible only in things like form, cadence, or endurance.[2]

We first see Chris Cahill sweating onto the track in a canary-yellow singlet with *Cal State* spelled out in loopy cursive right before she blows her chance to make the Olympic team at the 1976 trials in Eugene, Oregon. Soon she's whining to her dad-coach about her trailing leg, which comes off as a half-hearted excuse for her lackluster performance. Meanwhile, Tory Skinner watches Chris hurdle while holding a shot put in her hand, taking it all in. The scene feels ripped from a lesbian pulp novel.

Later, at a restaurant where many of the athletes are having dinner and drinks after the day's competition, Chris is unsteady on her feet and almost passes out from not eating. Tory swoops in to take care of her. They go back to Tory's place, where the two athletes drink and smoke marijuana and enjoy each other's company for quite some time based on the number of empty beer bottles that have accumulated in the scene. The buzzed talk turns to running and who has a killer instinct. Tory tells Chris that she choked and then goes on to suggest that her dad might not be the best choice for a coach because "sometimes knowing someone keeps you from knowing something that a total stranger could see right away." Chris replies, exasperated: "Hey, what is *this*?" Is the question about running? Something else? Tory says: "Who knows?" Both question and answer stretch out, "lightly, without trying to seize anything right away," as Barthes writes in *A Lover's Discourse*.[3] The answer is delayed by an awkward arm-wrestling contest entered into

and sustained with a lot of eye contact and heavy breathing that buys some time to decide where *this* is going. Later, as the runners lie naked in bed together, Chris checks out a scar over Tory's knee with a plastic pelican-shaped lamp, which is quite possibly the only afterglow scene in cinematic history featuring an illuminated seabird.

The casual marijuana use at the Olympic Trials in the film makes me think of Sha'Carri Richardson, the sprinter phenom who won so many American, running, and queer hearts in the 2021 trials. After winning the 100 meters, she raced up the stands to embrace the grandmother who raised her, with her coppery-orange hair dancing and her long nails, reminiscent of Flo-Jo, slicing through the wind. She thanked her girlfriend on social media and gave us a rainbow emoji. Later, we learned Richardson's biological mother had passed away and that she had been running with the weight of that loss. A reporter broke the news to her in a live interview, not caring how it might affect her, or her running. Richardson was thrown by this revelation on top of the pressure of the trials, so she smoked some pot. When the drug test revealed cannabis in her system, she lost her place on the Tokyo Olympic team and received a thirty-day ban from track. I imagine an alternative scenario where instead of a journalistic rush to write some clickbait article on an athlete's raw reaction, and in place of bureaucratic punishment, Richardson had received some tenderness and support. In this alternative reality, I like to think of her celebrating after the trials with her girlfriend, and as they enjoy each other's company, they know what *this* is, and they know something about what and who running can touch.

When I rewatch *Personal Best*, I find the most pleasure in the training montages. Chris and Tory running through the city, on the beach, and up enormous sand dunes to a soundtrack of drone music and heavy breathing—just legs, legs, legs free-wheeling in tiny shorts. I think of Anne Carson's line from *Eros, the Bittersweet*: "To be running breathlessly, but not yet arrived, is itself delightful, a suspended moment of hope."[4] I want to stay in the middle of the montage, in the practice, in the space of unfolding and refolding, but the film moves on.

The relationship between Tory and Chris is never named, but it isn't hard to get the picture. There's the pelican lamp, but then there's joyful grocery shopping and the domestic space; there's practicing and living together for three years; there's Tory dressed in a tweed blazer and jealousy at a party after a track meet when Chris gives a guy the bulk of her attention; there's the debossed leather training book for keeping track of workouts that Tory makes Chris for her birthday; and there's the public kiss at the party in thanks for the gift. Later there's a fight in a car before track practice when Chris says, "Jesus Christ, Tory, we're friends," after Tory suggests seeing other people. And then there's Tory shooting back: "Yeah, we may be friends, but every once in a while we also fuck each other."

Tory's bluntness cracks something open. The lovers fall back together for a while, but anyone watching knows the happy montages are coming to an end. There is a definitive breakup after Chris injures her knee while trying out some high jumping advice from Tory. Chris's mark was moved out too far; it's left ambiguous whether this was intentional or accidental. I tend toward the latter, but the coach takes the opportunity to sow mistrust between the athletes. Chris moves out of their shared home and works on her recovery while Tory takes off for the Pan Am Games. Soon thereafter, Chris is awkwardly sliding Tory into the category of ex-"roommate" when on a date with guy. As Chris diminishes their relationship, and as running gives way to rehab, the charge of the film fizzles out, and so too does my interest.

Thankfully, without too much time passing, running is reinstated, and as we see Chris in a solo training montage, my attention snaps back. More than anything, it's the voice-over that gets me, repeating the phrase: "It's the 800 and you're going to have to *run*." This moment strikes my half-miler's heart. The last event of the pentathlon and of the film is the 800 meters. This race, my race, will decide who makes the Olympic team.

The trials have brought Chris and Tory back into contact. They are no longer lovers, but they are caught up again in queer friendship and against the strict orders of Chris's coach. Going into the 800, Pooch Anderson, a runner who is unfortunately always a minor character in the film despite being the most talented, is in first place. Chris is in second place, followed by Charlene Benveniste in third, with Tory in fourth. Only three athletes qualify for a spot on the team. Chris comes up with a race strategy where, if it works, the points will add up so that both Tory and Chris will make the Olympic team: it is a competitive calculus that will cut Benveniste out of the podium. To make the team, Chris only needs to get third, but Tory needs to cross the line first. For Tory to win, Chris will need to burn off Benveniste, so she will have no kick at the end.

As we wait for the gun to go off, all the tension of Chekhov is bundled in the athletes' bodies lunging just behind the line. After the bang, there's a bit of jostling with shoulder and elbow contact as the runners move from their staggered starting lines to the inner lanes. Chris sets a blistering pace. Benveniste is going for the win to ensure that she qualifies, but Chris runs inside her, forcing her to run in the second lane by not giving her any space to cross over or to pass. Benveniste is kept outside, meaning she will run three to four meters farther for each lap. This is a risky and ambitious strategy, when every step counts. Tory's boxed in but finds a way through, her shaggy brown hair flopping rhythmically down the last stretch. Tory crosses the line first, then Pooch Anderson, then Chris, with Benveniste coming in fourth. Chris collapses, spent from the effort of exhausting Benveniste. Tory rushes to help her, and as she holds the languid body of her ex-lover, a little pietà is created on the infield.

Chris and Tory make the Olympic team, along with Pooch, who wins the pentathlon, but the whole effort of the race, and even of the four years of practice depicted in the film, falls a little flat since President Carter made the decision to boycott the Moscow games in response to the Soviet invasion of Afghanistan. The writer Ken Kesey famously called the 1980 trials the "Olympic Trials to Nowhere." A strange side effect of the boycott is how many actual athletes ended up being extras in *Personal Best*. Since they didn't have an Olympics to go to, they could add some sporting realness to Towne's film.

As a runner and a queer person, I don't find much to hang on to in *Personal Best*, even if it is fun to see Mariel Hemingway and Pat Donnelly sweaty, focused, and gay, at least for a little while. By contrast, when I first laid eyes on the cover of Team Dresch's album *Personal Best*, I saw the track team of my dreams. It foregrounds two queer runners crouched down on a track looking at each other in the ready position, about to race or make out, or maybe both. They are suited up in tall striped socks, baggy shorts, and sweatbands, with a whole line of other runners behind them who are similarly kitted out. For me, this was a reparative image. These runners were dressed how I did in the late 1990s and early 2000s, when I went running, out dancing, or even to my job right after college working as a digital cartographer. It meant the world to me to see my world represented in culture. The songs on *Personal Best* are ferocious but also tender; they are about crushes, friendship, love, and raging against everything that gets in the way of queer flourishing. The band is even named in the spirit of queer friendship after one of its members, Donna Dresch, the "captain" of the team. It's hard to stress how important this album was for me. When I first heard Team Dresch, its music made me feel like I was in a montage, like I was gearing up for something, like things were going somewhere. Today, as I listen to *Personal Best* as a kind of research for this handbook and while I do my stretches to get ready to run, I give a runner's nod to past Lindseys warming up, I touch a space of queer history, and I feel a montage coming on.

In Training for the Boston Marathon

My mom is sitting on the steps of the redbrick house I grew up in. She's wearing running shoes with a navy Swoosh, royal blue shorts, and a T-shirt in that perfect shade of classic-sweatshirt heather gray with the words "In training for the Boston Marathon" printed in red on the chest. This is one of my favorite photographs of my mother, although I'm not sure she would like it very much. She's not looking glamorous, like someone who knows how to be photographed, as she often does. I love this snapshot because it captures something of her spirit that other family photos miss. I was eight years old and behind the camera, and so part of what I like about it is how she is looking at me. In the photo my mother is the age I am now.

My mom wasn't planning to run Boston. She had never even considered it, but she did run regularly and competed in local 5K races. My dad brought the T-shirt back from a business trip, with Harvard shirts for my brother and me, but Harvard never captured my imagination like the Boston Marathon did.

It wasn't just running the marathon that appealed to me; it was also all the practice that I imagined it would take, the fervor of it.

I searched everywhere trying to find this photo of my mom, which I've misplaced. I wanted to include it in this handbook. I didn't want this to be like Roland Barthes's winter garden photograph of his mother, the ghostly image that haunts *Camera Lucida*, that image that is just for the author. I wanted you to see how I could be inspired to run by how the late afternoon light of a summer day hits a runner, my mother, fit and strong and smiling at me. As I reflect on this image and my running practice, I'm certain that this longing to run is caught up in love, for my mom, for the soft cotton of T-shirts, and for endurance projects.

The Boston Marathon is not like most races where you simply pay your entry fee and show up. Or even like other popular marathons, such as Chicago or New York City, where, unless you are a professional or at the tippity-top of the amateurs, you enter a lottery because the race frequently reaches capacity. I tried for five years before I was selected from the tens of thousands of people wanting to run through New York's five boroughs and to finish in Central Park, but that's nothing compared with a lifetime of wanting to try my luck in Boston. There are only two official ways into the Boston Marathon: the first is to run fast in another sanctioned marathon, to score what runners call a BQ, or Boston qualifying time, and the second is to raise a heap of money for a charity. The BQ cutoff times are set by age, with about ten minutes added for every decade going up to the eighties. Qualifying times also change through time, as the pool of runners gets more competitive. A person's BQ time is good for two years, then expires. Runners who can lay down a quick enough marathon time to earn a BQ are generally considered to be in the top 10 percent of amateur runners. Still, a BQ is often not enough to get you in due to the sheer number of people who want to run this race and the field size limitations, so a marathoner typically has to run a time several minutes faster than the minimum requirement in order to be selected for Boston.

I qualified for Boston once after landing a good enough time in the Baltimore Marathon. As I was training, I delighted in running in my mom's T-shirt, which she had finally given to me after decades of my coveting it. To those who saw me wearing it on the street it might have looked like bragging, but to me the shirt was also a family heirloom, a material representation of a love for my mother and for running, and part of a uniform for a training montage waiting to happen that I carried with me from Tennessee to South Carolina to DC to Brooklyn, and to all the various places I traveled and trained.

I was wearing this shirt when I had the worst run of my life. It happened on one of those days when a combination of having too much work to do and a feeling of afternoon drag had me thinking: I should go on a run, I could use a break, I'll feel better, more energized, but maybe I should finish grading these papers first, get out a few more emails, or just lie on the couch, watch TV, and take a rest day. In the end I decided to go, promising myself I would only do a short one. I set out to do a kind of city training run that I call "lights," where I'd go for a relatively set amount of time, switching directions when the stoplights changed, often making decisions quickly on the yellows. The constraint calls for running at least the intended time, but this time is often extended because you have to get home (or where you started from) by running, no walking allowed! It is a good way to trick yourself into running a little more.

About twenty minutes into my run, I was crossing the busy intersection of Flushing and Bushwick Avenues in Brooklyn. Halfway across, I had the sensation that something was not right. I turned and instantly understood that I would quickly meet the grill of a Honda CR-V. The thought was sharp, like a huge blade slicing through me: I have never been so afraid in my life. I thought I would be killed. The vehicle punched me in the ribs and knocked me down. A split second later, I felt an immense pressure, but no pain: the front tire and the weight of the vehicle rolling over my legs. I had a panicked thought: "Did that happen?!" I didn't have long to wait for an answer to my question, as the back tire arrived nearly immediately to confirm my suspicion. It was hard for me to take in what had just happened. As I went down, my head slapped the pavement, which could have added to my confusion. Even now, some things about the accident are fuzzy, while other parts are clear in my memory. I'm still not sure what caused it, if I timed the light wrong, or if the small SUV that hit me jumped the turn signal.

In the movies, when someone gets hits by a car, they always sail over the top. This was not something I ever questioned, but now I've learned that this is "movie magic." Sometimes we go up and over, and sometimes we go down and below. Maybe it's too gruesome to see us go under, but that is just where I went.

After the CR-V ran over me, I found myself alone and exposed, a wounded animal stuck to the road. I heard yelling: "Help! Help!" Although the voice was coming from me, it seemed to arrive from somewhere outside of myself, or outside of time, as in a dream. My glasses had been broken by the fall, but I hadn't realized it yet. Before I noticed them, in two pieces, out of my reach, I saw my shoes about six feet away. A terrible fear raced through me: "Oh, God, please don't let my feet still be in my Asics."[1] I was relieved when I saw them at the bottoms of my legs, still in their socks, but I couldn't feel them. My body was too drowned in fear chemicals to even know whether I had been dismembered without verifying my completeness through vision. On this day, one of the things I learned was that you can get hit so hard that your shoes will fly off from the impact. I'm still not sure what it takes to knock your socks off, but this is knowledge I can do without.

As I lay in the street, a skinny hipster guy approached me and tried to pick me up. As he reached down, I thought he was the most beautiful person I had ever seen. What all the action rom-com movies show you is true: when you are in an extreme situation and afraid for your life and someone tries to help you, they are bathed in a golden light and appear to be almost otherworldly attractive. But just as he was about to touch me, onlookers started yelling: "Stop! Don't move her!" and "Her back might be broken!" As I watched him retract his arms, a wave of desperation rippled through me. I wanted this stranger to save me; I was lying in a busy street, unsure if I could move, and worried that if I didn't move, any second another car would

finish me off. Soon the EMTs appeared, and as I was strapped to a hard wooden board the first twinges of pain arrived in my ribs. Free of immediate danger, I began to worry if I would be OK, and whether I would be able to pay for the ambulance if I was. Such is the brutality of the American health care system that even in times like these the fear of economic ruin enters the scene.

The EMT closest to me who lifted me up had a tattoo of Saint Sebastian on his forearm. Saint Sebastian, the gayest saint, the saint of Derek Jarman, and the saint of endurance—my saint, if I had to pick—gave me some comfort. I wanted so badly for this beautiful, burly redheaded bear of a man to hold my hand, but I didn't know how to ask for it. I lay there in the ambulance, focusing on Saint Sebastian dancing on my ginger savior's arm as I was peppered with questions, first about my body, then about my social and romantic life. The body questions: "Could you be pregnant?" Then: "Can you feel this?" I was asked as someone touched my legs, my back, my midsection. All I could eke out was "I don't know, I don't know, I don't know. Is that bad?" No one answered. I thought I might be paralyzed.

The next set of questions were repeated over the following hours. The first few aimed to establish my coherence: "What is your name? What is your address? Do you know what day it is? Who is the president?" These were then followed by "Are you pregnant? Is there any chance you could be pregnant?" And, finally, by the relationship questions: "Is there anyone we can call? Do you have a roommate? Are you married? Do you live with a partner?" These questions hit me at a time of divine singleness, when I had emerged from what I felt were tragic and mismatched romantic relationships. I was living alone, blissfully, in a sun-filled railroad apartment, finishing my PhD, teaching writing and social theory, and running marathons. I had lots of friends I could call, but the only numbers I had memorized were my mother's in Tennessee, the house phones of my childhood friends, and the number of one ex-girlfriend, who was the absolute last person I wanted to see on that day. I had set out to run in shorts and my "In Training for the Boston Marathon" T-shirt with only a key to my apartment. All the numbers that would connect me to people who cared about me, who could come get me, were sitting inside my cell phone on my desk next to a to-do list that still had unchecked boxes for a short tempo run and first-year writing papers to grade.

As soon as the ambulance arrived at the hospital, the speed of everything accelerated. Hospital staff wheeled me down a long corridor, which looked just like the pale thresholds from every hospital drama I have ever watched. I was living the scene of patient arrival, lying on a bed with wheels, as nurses hurried alongside like bobsledders at the beginning of a race, but without ever jumping on. I was looking up watching one huge ceiling light after another in a bright, dizzying fast-paced haze. I was taken to a room where I was the only patient. A team of eight or ten surrounded me; someone was taking my blood pressure; a couple of people were asking *the questions*. I was touched everywhere, hands seeming to cover every inch of me, while someone cut off my clothes with huge scissors and another person placed sticky electrodes on my chest. My best running shorts, black Adidas with three stripes down the side, a gray sports bra, and yes, my family heirloom "In Training for the Boston Marathon" shirt were all sliced off my body. Later, I found out that someone took the cheap Casio watch from my wrist and set it aside for me. It had a scratch down its face but still kept perfect time. I do not know what happened to my shoes or my glasses.

A nurse helped me into a hospital gown the color of periwinkle, and a thin white sheet was placed over the length of me. I was roughly X-rayed, with the technician jerking my limbs around without telling me which way he was going, sometimes putting his knee into my side looking for leverage as he climbed on the platform that held my body. I was fearful that he would cause me more injury. I still had no idea the extent of the damage done to me. After imaging, I was returned to the trauma unit and things slowed down. Nurses periodically monitored me as I lay staring at the ceiling for hours, scared and cold, but happy to be there, to be anywhere. I worried about the classes I was supposed to teach the next day and whether I would be able to run or even walk again.

Several hours later, a doctor came by and told me: "If you can stand up, we are going to release you soon." She sped off before I had a chance to ask any questions. Standing seemed highly unlikely to me after what I had experienced. Also, my glasses had been broken, my clothes destroyed and removed, and I had no money, no shoes, and no idea even where I was beyond Elmhurst Hospital. After the doctor left my bedside, my brain was racing with this new information. I asked a nurse where we were, and he said "Queens." I followed with: "Are we far from Bushwick, Brooklyn?" He had no idea. I needed some advice, so I asked him what I was supposed to do if I was released, and he said: "We could probably get you a metro card." I imagined what this would look like, struggling down the metro steps, naked underneath a thin hospital gown, my legs raw, bloody, and full of bits of road. Concussed and without my glasses, I would have to get really close to the map to see what connections I needed to make to get home, nearly pressing my nose to it. I wondered if, when the train came, I would be able to get a seat, if fellow riders would give me that, and then I wondered if I even could sit down, or if I would want to.

More time passed, with these new things to consider. Then the doctor swung back around to ask: "Is there someone we can call who could come get you?" I repeated the story: I was running, it's 2012 and no one remembers phone numbers anymore. I had already tried to explain this to the EMTs, to one nurse, and then another, and another, that I had friends who would come help me, but I would need a way to email them. The message I was implicitly receiving was "You will die forgotten and alone, but if you are lucky, first you will hobble out of this hospital by yourself and take the subway back to your lonely existence."

If only I could send a message to my friends! I was distressed. It would be great if I could stand, but the subway seemed unworkable. I made a plan that, if released, I would ask the hospital to call me a cab, then I would explain to the cabbie what had happened, and once I got to my three-floor walkup I would climb the stairs, get my wallet, come back down and pay, and then climb the stairs again to get myself back up to my apartment. Thinking about all those steps in this state was like imagining climbing Everest, but it was the only option I could see.

As my brain was spinning this potential plan, the doctor came back around and coolly slid me her cell phone, saying, "I'm not supposed to do this, but email your friends." She swifted off as quickly as she had arrived, and with a golden light surrounding her too. Now . . . how to compose this email? I had been at the hospital for hours. I left for my run around four and it was now ten o'clock at night. I hoped that someone would get the message. I loaded up about twenty friends to receive this email with the subject line: "Help!! For real emergency." Then: "I was hit by a car while running. I'm OK but need someone to come get me. Elmhurst hospital" followed by the phone number of the trauma unit. I had to add the "for real" because I'm sure that I have sent countless emails like "Help! Emergency! I can't write this chapter and I need to drink beers in the park with you ASAP." Soon the doctor came by and told me that my friends Jane and Nancy were on their way. This news brought a colossal relief. Jane and Nancy are two of my oldest friends and absolutely the sort of people you would want in an emergency. They have cared for me and sheltered me through many personal challenges, heartbreaks, and disasters, always with a comfortable couch, wonderful snacks, and good humor.

When they walked into the room, toting an old sweatshirt, cargo pants, and a pair of sneakers, I knew I would be some sort of OK. I was so overwhelmed by my feeling of rescue that I had forgotten the doctor was going to try to get me vertical. She called it a "standing test," and when the moment came, she told me to take it slowly, and I laughed that that was all I could do. One foot on the cold floor, then the other, I pushed off from the bed, and there I was standing, even if a little shaky.

I felt like I had been converted into one of those true believers who had hands laid on them in one of the wilder televangelist shows that my grandmother watched. It was only then that I learned I had no broken bones but some cracked ribs, a lot of contusions, a concussion, a nasty case of road rash, and two oily, gritty black tire marks set into the back of my legs to prove this wasn't just a nightmare. Later there would be MRIs, physical therapy, and pugilistic phone calls with insurance companies, but for now I was to be released into the care of my friends.

I had no idea what this episode would mean for me and for my running life. At first, I simply felt lucky to be alive. As I contemplated how to deal with the gravel embedded in my raw and badly swollen legs, along with the tire tread tattoos across my hamstrings, friends volunteered to teach my classes for a couple of weeks. People came over night after night bringing food and hanging out for hours: my apartment was an epicenter of warm affects and queer care. Jane and Nancy brought a huge amount of red grapes, which help skin heal. I still crave the curried tomato soup Linsey Ly made. I think it was Monica who brought the whiskey. In these early days after the accident, I watched tons of TV and movies, developed a crush on Lady Mary from *Downton Abbey*, and cried excessively, often at odd things. Still bleeding into Jane's old army green cargo pants, I cruised marathon websites and profiles on the online dating site OKCupid. I imagined running again and going on dates, when the swelling subsided and I could fit back into my jeans and bend over to tie my shoes without whimpering. The most daunting task was taking a bath, so I put it off for as long as I felt I could. My legs were raw and pink, and still striated with the stuff of the road. Finally, I screwed up my courage. As I lowered myself into the water, the pain was otherworldly; my body sang with it. Soon the bath took on a muddy-gray tint. When the water drained, little bits of gravel that my skin had emitted were collected in the drain catcher. I fished them out and laid them on the ledge of the sink, leaving them there for a few days as evidence, material reminders that this wild thing had happened.

Running the Risk Of

When I was able to return to teaching after getting run over, my students welcomed me back warmly, wincing as they watched me struggle with the stairs on campus. A student in my first-year writing class made me a get-well cartoon of an anthropomorphized bow tie—my constant classroom accessory—who falls victim to an evil tire but comes out on the other side of it skipping and whistling a tune, clearly in the pink of life. Although I was not skipping yet, and my legs were still badly bruised and swollen, the gesture buoyed me. I could feel myself stretch out a little again.

Still in pain and limping, I went out on a date with someone who was a hairstylist/performance artist and was also in a women's healing circle. She told me that she thought getting run over was the way the universe was telling me to slow down. I relayed this story to my friend Asifa, who said, "I mean, on the other hand, you could say you weren't running fast enough so you should really pick up the pace in your life," which is why we are friends. I went to physical therapy and threw myself into my rehab exercises, and within a couple of months I could ride my bicycle. I rode it to what I call a "look see," which is what I call meeting someone in person whom you've been chatting with on the internet, to see if you want to go on an actual date with them. I met Jessi for brunch at Pies and Thighs in Williamsburg; we looked; we saw. As we ate our slices of pie, I told my story of getting run over, making a little play on the table with a saltshaker (me) and a ketchup bottle (Honda). When my narrative wore down, Jessi looked under the table to get a peek at my legs, which were sticking out of the long navy shorts my grandmother called "Bermudas." We decided to go on a date. Soon, we fell in love and the cadence of our life together began.

I started running again. On my first run back I returned to the intersection of my accident: not all environments of touch that we turn and return to are gentle. I felt that by running through this space I would regain something of myself that had been lost, a certain toughness of spirit. I was plot driven, sure that this exercise would be the right move for the next chapter of my life. As I took a few steps to the other side, I experienced a splitting sensation, a feeling of bilocation: I imagined one Lindsey upright and running safely, and another Lindsey laid flat on the asphalt on her way to becoming a human speed bump. If you asked me, as I crossed the street, whether the position of my body remained running, I would have said, "I don't know"; if you asked me if the position of my running body would change with time, I would have responded, "I don't know"; if you asked me whether I was knocked to the street, I would again have said, "I don't know"; and if you questioned whether I was in motion, I would have replied, "I don't know."[1]

I only became sure of the position of my body when I made it to the next block, where a light stopped me and I could catch my breath. I was shaking so wildly that I stopped my run and walked home.

I used to be a real cowboy in the streets, running against the lights, zigzagging wherever I saw fit, confident that I could make it to the other side, that I could beat the cars, the buses, the bicycles, your mother, whoever, but I am now cautious when I run, and even when I walk, in cities. Whenever I see CR-V on the back of a Honda, I imagine my body as the hyphen between the letters. I never cross unless I have a green light or a little illuminated person signaling my time to go, even when the space seems clear to do so. And even though my first run back was through the scene of my accident, I have not run it again since. I take pains to avoid it when I'm visiting friends in Brooklyn. The trauma took some time to settle in, but when it did, it set up house. Just thinking of that space in the center of the road makes me feel small and nauseous. I still experience a wave of fear when I run through intersections, not always, but often, imagining my body crunching under the wheels of a car. These moments are not memory, although they are certainly triggered by memory, because when I have this feeling, I'm not sure I get up again. I don't think I'll ever develop a competence in my runner-brain to keep up with the velocity that trauma travels. I miss exercising my abandon, but it, too, has another mode of ongoingness: I carry it with me in my narrative repertoire. Getting run over and making it through is a trauma story. Rare for the genre, it is a story that is fun to tell at parties.

Courage, or The Paris Marathon

I didn't run the Boston Marathon that I had been training for when I was hit and run over, but I had one more year in which my time from the Baltimore Marathon would make me eligible. That year passed too, as my plans changed again, this time because of something far nicer than a trip to a trauma hospital in Queens: an invitation to go to the University of Caen in Normandy as a visiting professor. I decided to run the Paris Marathon instead. I tried to keep up my training, but it was difficult to manage when unusual March snowstorms made the streets and sidewalks too slippery to run and when new obligations and invitations had me distracted. On days when I couldn't get out, I did stretches and core exercises in my small, window-filled room looking out onto campus, as I watched college students slip and slide up a little hill on their way to and from classes. I worked on my lectures for the Space and Society Center, wrote an essay about snow globes and memory, and waited to hear about a job that I interviewed for in Buffalo. I didn't worry too much about the marathon. I knew that I could run the distance, barring some unexpected injury, but I was not sure until the invitation to Caen that I would get the chance to be a professor. I wanted to enjoy it while I could.

I ran poorly in the Paris Marathon. It was my worst marathon by far. I was undertrained but still managing to run somewhat decently until I tweaked my knee by stepping awkwardly on a cobblestone around mile nine. Each step after that caused a flash of bright pain to shoot through me, blurring my other senses. The sights, sounds, and smells of the city of Paris, the colorful getups of the runners in front of me, and the spring sky all blended into a hazy and oversaturated color field. I could barely taste the little packet of running gummies I ate mostly to cheer myself up and to give me something else to focus on besides my screaming knee. I was in what runners call "the pain cave," a movable metaphorical architecture of misery that surrounds and encloses while creating a feeling of distance from the world at large.

I stopped to stretch and engage in a little self-assessment. I found I could do a kind of hop-limp-running-esque movement that would move me along slightly quicker and take some pressure off my knee, which was already starting to swell. This worked for a while, but around mile seventeen, I could feel the toll my awkward running was taking on other parts of my compensating body. My hip began to protest in a serious way, and my neck and shoulders were scrunched up and achy. I had to stop and stretch once again and reorganize my appendages. I considered dropping out. I had no strategy at this point. The hopping was simply no longer going to work, and it was time to move forward one step at a time however I could manage. This might have been the ugliest running I have ever done, and there is a deep well of ugliness to draw from.

I still remember the crestfallen feeling I had when a runner dressed in an enormous foam Eiffel Tower costume passed by, making it look easy. Then a couple of miles later, a feeling even worse, when a joggler—a person juggling while jogging—overtook me while keeping three colorful beanbags in the air in a cascading pattern.[1] The scenes of a marathon can be surreal, especially when your senses are going crazy from pain and exhaustion. As James McWilliams writes in an essay on the Boston Marathon: "Marathoners can't plagiarize."[2] Although, if you've ever run one from the middle of the pack or farther back, you'll know scenes like this are not uncommon. Like anthropologists coming home from the field, marathoners often begin their stories with "I swear I saw this."[3]

In the last miles, cheers of "Courage!" from the Parisians lining the streets broke through the muffling walls of my pain cave and propelled me through my agony. Knowing I would get to the end lifted my spirits, even as my form continued to devolve. When I finally finished, I wrapped myself up in one of the silvery heat blankets, sometimes called "space blankets," that are handed out after races and give the wearer the look of a human baked potato.[4] I slunk to the metro with my medal around my neck, and occasionally someone said "Courage!" to me. If they had that wrung-out look of a marathon runner experiencing not-running, I said "Courage" back with a little runner's nod of respect; otherwise I said "Merci." Looking back now, it is pretty amazing that I could run at all considering that a Honda had driven over my legs less than a year before, but during those miserable seventeen miles slogging through one of the most beautiful cities on earth, I had forgotten all about that.

Jessi came to visit me a day after the marathon so we could spend a week together. As I hobbled along and then gradually regained my ability to walk without limping, we encountered a lot of political activism that perplexed us, including a group of shirtless men in pastel shorts hoping to protect "the family" through bare-chested shouting and homosociality. Pro-gay and antigay messages were chalked on the sidewalks, alerting us that there was a big vote coming up to determine whether gay couples could marry and adopt children. For the most part, this washed over us as we walked around blissed out on being in love and in Paris together. Coming from New York City, where no one cares too much what you do, as long as it doesn't slow them down, we were surprised to hear an entire bar clap and cheer "Courage!" as we walked home hand in hand after dinner one night. We were making a political statement without being aware of it. I was having quite a courageous week in Paris, simply by doing all the things I always do.

Runner's High

Running gives me a combined feeling of calm, focus, and euphoria that is difficult for me to find almost anywhere else. Part of this is chemical: sometimes when a person runs for long enough, the running body produces a cocktail of endogenous chemicals that can alter mood and sense perception, including beta-endorphins, opioids with a chemical structure similar to morphine; beta-phenylethylamine, which acts as a central nervous system stimulant and has a chemical structure akin to amphetamines; and anandamide, a fatty acid neurotransmitter known as a cannabinoid that induces feelings of pleasure. This trio helps the body handle pain and heightens alertness and mobility in the case of danger while simultaneously creating feelings of happiness and lightness, the constellation of sensations known as "runner's high."

When I'm high from running, perceptions come together in a reverie: the weather, the light, and the forest floor or the city sidewalk seem to conspire with my body to make running

feel like the best thing in the world. With my senses heightened the world itself seems supercharged: in spring, the grass greens even brighter; in summer, limbs unfettered by jackets and tights relish the heat; in autumn, the fallen leaves crunch with a pleasure that travels from my feet up my spine; and in winter, the freshness and freedom of being warm outside when moving wins over the chilly start to the run. Once I hit this register of pleasure, running remains in my body hours after I've finished and in memory for much longer. The memory keeps me motivated and chasing after that feeling of easiness in the run. To me, runner's high feels like being in love or finding out that someone I admire thinks my sentences are beautiful.

If I can give myself over to running, thoughts and feelings come in waves, like how dreams fade into one another, or how time passes in some cinema, where plot is less important than atmosphere, colors, and textures. Long runs trigger an inner experience of movement; sensing becomes more subtle, and interpretation is less subject to restraint or regulation. When I'm immersed in a run, the soft cadence of my shoes hitting the ground, the tone of my rhythmic breathing, the dull clicking sound of my apartment keys hitting against each other in the little pocket of my shorts all work together to put me in meditative and imaginative zones. If I avoid looking at my watch too much, I can find a state of untimeliness, where time swells and dilutes; sometimes there is a sense of infinity, and the feeling that I could run like this forever. In these moments, I float, I flow, I dissolve: "I am nowhere gathered together."[1] When I'm running like this, thoughts and ideas do not usually sharpen to a point, but rather spool out like a cassette tape gone rogue.

I wind up these loose thoughts later with a pencil at my desk, where I transform them into something lyrical, something I can run with.

These feelings of lightening and loosening come most often when I'm doing LSD, which is runner shorthand for long slow distance, a form of aerobic running practice generally attributed to the German physician and coach Dr. Ernst van Aaken. Although, van Aaken never called it LSD; he named his coaching method *Waldnieler Dauerlauf*, meaning "Waldniel endurance run," after the village where he lived. The American runner and writer Joe Henderson coined the expression "LSD" in 1969, effectively popularizing and rebranding the method in his training handbook *Long Slow Distance*. From there, LSD was taken up by competitive runners as well as the growing number of recreational joggers looking for exercise highs and for endurance. Henderson didn't consider LSD a training method per se; he thought of it as a practice and a "whole way of looking at the sport."[2] People started to call him the Timothy Leary of running, although he waved off this association.

Henderson advocated running gently as an antidote to what he called the PTA, or "Pain, Torture, and Agony," school of running.[3] Long slow distance runs are meant to increase a capacity for endurance while not being overly taxing. They are ideally done at one to three minutes slower per mile than your 10K racing pace, at a clip where you could comfortably hold a conversation. If you run alone, try singing to yourself, and if that makes you winded, ease up a little.

While both long slow distance and the narcotic commonly known as acid that shares the acronym have been used for recreational and spiritual reasons, only running improves cardiovascular health, thermoregulatory function, mitochondrial energy production, and the oxidative capacity of skeletal muscle and is known to be addictive. Take caution because, once you start running LSD, you might want to do it all the time, but if you do too much too soon, you can easily become exhausted or injured. A good general guide to building endurance is to increase your mileage no more than 10 percent per week; avoid running your max distance or pace on every run; make sure to have some easy recovery runs between hard efforts; and, unless racing, always hold something in reserve. Your legs will get used to running more and more; your heart will too.

I like to find that sweet spot where I feel a sense of depletion when I finish a run, but not one that's so deep that I can't go again the following day. Similar to my writing practice, I try to leave off knowing I can pick up the threads in the next session with new energy and a sense of coherence. I find that it helps to make a schedule, but to allow for flexibility. One day you might find yourself full of running and you'll want to go for a little longer than you planned. Another day life might get in the way of living and you are too tired to go at all. To avoid burnout, give yourself these allowances on occasion. While doing long runs is the key to building endurance, don't be afraid to microdose LSD or take what I call a "languid short distance" run. A microdose of LSD is running superslow whenever you feel tired from running practice or the pinch of life. You won't experience the full effects of LSD with a short, slow run, and it's unlikely that you'll hit a radically altered state of experience, but it can still take the edge off a day.

It's important to note that long slow distance running can induce distorted thoughts, feelings, and awareness of one's surroundings. It is not uncommon to hallucinate during the miles of long-distance training runs or races. I find that I hallucinate most often when my runner's high starts to ebb, and that most often these visions are helpful. The hallucinations I experience have varied over the years. While some I have had only once, others are frequent visitors—my most persistent hallucination is of a smaller version of myself who sits inside my head in a space that resembles an airline cockpit. During these experiences, the tiny me, which looks through my eyes, as if a windshield, becomes the agential me, the one in control. In these hallucinations, my diminutive self is busy at work, moving the limbs of my full-size body, which it operates with a series of levers tipped with bright colors. The tiny me does not feel the pounding of my legs on the pavement, heavy with fatigue; the little Lindsey in my head is tireless and carries us through.

Let's Let Our Running Be Real

There are times when my running is almost effortless, when I am running completely within myself, coasting along in the space of good feeling the psychologist Mihaly Csikszentmihalyi calls "flow."[1] And there are times when my running feels detached, a painful torment, when below the waist my legs feel shredded into disparate parts swinging like the leather fringe on a cowboy jacket. There are runs when stabbing pains slice through my abdomen and runs when it seems like my guts are dissolving into one angry mass of goo. On some runs my Achilles tendon feels like it is being repeatedly hit by a mallet. Others have ended (or should have ended) with ankle sprains where the joint rolls over, interrupting the flow of the run, like a mark of punctuation out of place. And there are runs when my hip flexors feel like they are hooked up to electricity going haywire, delivering shocks intermittently that make me jump with pain; on these runs I feel I'm a participant in an experi-

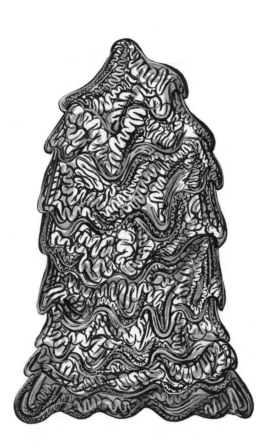

ment driven by an unseen sadist, as if the shocks in a Stanley Milgram experiment were for real.

As J. B. Strasser and Laurie Becklund write in *Swoosh*, a history of Nike: "Every sport has an emotional edge."[2] Running's emotional edge rides the line between a love of endurance and an interest in feeling what happens when you are (nearly) breaking down. In *Running Is Your Life*, the documentary about Lasse Virén, the narrator intones: "All runners are carrying with them pain, all-encompassing agony, uncertainty, and foggy consciousness. . . . Only the knowledge that this soon will be over gives the runners strength to finish the race." In poet and runner Thomas Gardner's memoir about everyday practice and running through grief, he writes: "At some point, in almost every race, you get lost. You open your eyes and realize you're in trouble. Your heart rate rises, your concentration buckles, and you're suddenly flailing around inside, with no landmark save for a familiar hatred of yourself and the ego that made you line up and race. You slow down and turn on yourself."[3] And even in an otherwise blissed-out account of running, Fred Rohé concedes in his 1974 handbook, *The Zen of Running*: "Sometimes running is suffering intentionally for the sake of seeing, sometimes running is resisting and suffering unintentionally because we are human beings. Let's not make our running a fantasy, let's let our running be real."[4] As these examples show, Rohé is not alone in this admission or in his call to honesty. Every running memoir and handbook, even those that elevate running to near gospel or nirvana, admit that running sometimes feels terrible, and that it can even cause the runner to question the very practice they love, so I too have made concessions to the genre.

Some runs I never want to end, and some runs can be an excruciating slog; sometimes they are the same run. But when people ask me, "If it can be so awful, why do you run?" or "What if I told you I read an article that said running is the absolute worst thing you could do for your body?"—in these moments I think of Lauren Berlant's line "There is nothing more alienating than having one's pleasures disputed by someone with a theory."[5] And like Barthes's lover, "I counter whatever doesn't work" in my love of running "with the affirmation of what is worthwhile. This stubbornness is love's protest."[6]

On Hitting the Wall and
Writer's Block

Hitting the wall is the running equivalent of writer's block. Neither of these phrases comes close to describing what these states actually look or feel like. The words conjure something stationary and still: one object unable to move another, full stop. But if you've ever hit the wall or experienced writer's block, you know that to be in one of these states is to be flailing about, a person coming apart, losing *it*. For the writer or the runner experiencing these feelings, even if there is an illusion of calm on the outside, everything inside can feel desperate and wild. A scene of writer's block often finds the writer sitting at their desk, fingers poised on the keyboard, or flipping through a notebook for cues, then looking out the window pensively, maybe turning to social media or obsessively cooking or cleaning for distraction. The writer might have anxiety, a crisis of confidence, a breakdown in their posture or good eating and sleeping habits; they might neglect their students or loved ones, or turn all their focus toward them, giving them everything, while attempting to ignore the work that gnaws at their sense of what is to be done. Even stasis, for the writer, is not an effortless state. And for the runner who hits the wall, who is barely shuffling along, listing at odd angles, or stiff-legged zombie jogging, stretched well beyond their reserves, the feeling is not singular; it is hitting the wall over and over again. The alternative running argot for this state—bonking—might be more apt.

When a runner bonks, they can sometimes still move forward, slowly, weirdly, even as their body or mind, or sometimes both, stalls. This might seem like a slightly more pleasant state than the blocked writer because there is a bit of progress, but there is no value in competition here. In both cases, the danger of scoring what runners call a "DNF," or "did not finish," hangs in the balance. If you've ever been blocked in the weeks before a writing deadline, trashing each and every line you've written, feeling bereft of ideas and inspiration, and unable to will a single good paragraph into being, then you know this feeling. Or if you've ever hit the wall in a marathon with the finish line three miles away, as I did in the New York City Marathon, you too know this special flavor of experience in which the mind simply cannot get ideas to come or the legs to understand how to go faster, and in extreme cases how to go at all. And if you're still able to think in these states, which is a big if, you find yourself not sure how or if you'll make it to the finish, although this is all you want—to be a runner experiencing not-running, or a writer experiencing not-writing—while still making it to the end of what you've set out to do.

The wild thing is that, for me, this feeling seldom lasts, and almost as soon as I've managed to hit "send" on my manuscript or eaten something and taken a shower, my brain and body are unblocked and unbonked. I am recovered and whirling, planning the next book or marathon, or at the very least an essay or a 10K. I know lots of other writers and runners who are like this too.

When I think of this quick shift from exhaustion to the desire to practice, I think of the 1984 LA Olympic marathon and how it imprinted possibility in me. I've already mentioned the dominating run by Joan Benoit, who still looked sprightly even at the end, but there was also the Swiss runner Gabriela Andersen-Schiess, who suffered badly from heat prostration in the last miles. This, too, was an example of what can happen from running. On her final lap around the stadium track, Andersen-Schiess staggers, leans to the left, and zigzags from lane to lane. She stops periodically to hold her head and crush her hat in her hand like she's mad at it. Many people were outraged she wasn't pulled from the track, she looked so awful. It's painful to watch her suffer the four minutes and fifty-five seconds it takes her to complete the lap with doctors just on the side of her trying to determine if she could go on. Finally, she makes it across the finish line, collapses in a heap, and is carried off on a stretcher with socks stained from blood and from sweat mixed with the dye of her burgundy Adidas shoes.

At her press conference the next morning, Andersen-Schiess casually describes being in a fugue state for the last two miles of the race. She is pushed by the reporters to heroize her finish but resists it at every turn. She states simply: "It's not the first time this has happened. It's not uncommon in a long hot race that people have troubles. After two hours [from finishing] I was fine." And the part that devastates me is that she feels the need to declare: "It happens to men too."[1] The press conference ends as she tells reporters how she went on a run that very morning, how she felt good, and how she's training for another race.

Repetitive Stress

What do you do when your regular practice of running, your stress reliever, causes a repetitive stress injury?

What do you do when you're not able to turn to the practices you use to even yourself out? What happens when you can't do the things that make you recognizable to yourself and others? Do you swim? Do you work? Do you drink? Do you find ways to tie yourself into knots because you feel that you should have been able to notice the signs and pull back before you ended up in this place where you just can't go anymore?

I do.

In an essay called "The Lonely Marathon," Kevin Lewis writes that running gives "the opportunity, if not the necessity, of more closely monitoring the complex Gestalt of the bodily processes under stress than in virtually any other sport available to the mass public."[1] It's a paradox that while most runners become attuned to their bodies, many of us also cling to the antipodes of awareness. We ignore signals, misinterpret them, run through them, and sometimes relish our pain. We create an architecture of feeling to house our suffering, a mobile home we call a "pain cave." We congratulate ourselves on our abilities to decorate these caves with our perseverance. This ongoingness becomes part of the story we tell about ourselves as runners, and the stories that others tell about us in turn.

Putting the sometimes grotesque celebration of suffering aside for a moment, pain, or at least discomfort, is part of running, like any demanding physical activity. It can be difficult to identify the point where the body is breaking down to an extent that it will not heal quickly. It is not easy to tell when the stress we've put on ourselves is too great. Runners, like most people, are not particularly good at paying attention to the complex gestalts of our bodies under the stresses of living. Below are three moments, chosen out of many possibilities, where in stubborn adherence to doing what I have always done I was injured by repetitively stressing my body in an attempt to deal with other stresses and to remain recognizable to myself and how I imagine others recognize me.

During my junior year of college track, I developed a stress fracture in my navicular, a small, boat-shaped bone in the top of the middle part of the foot. I ran the last two months of the season with the fracture. The pain was terrible, especially during races when I wore my track spikes. I remember that when I raced, I felt like my foot would break in half. But I worried that if I gave up track, I would have *nothing*.

When I was in my early thirties and training for a marathon, I had a bad ankle sprain. My anxiety was ramping up as I missed training, so I tried to double down, running twice in a day sometimes, trying to claw back the miles I thought I had missed. I quickly sprained the other ankle, the right one this time. Not too bad, I thought. So, too soon again, I was back out there. Then I resprained the left one. Months of healing awaited me, instead of the five or six weeks it would have taken to heal and rehabilitate the first injury. But I was convinced that I *needed* running in order to finish my PhD.

In my first year living in Vancouver, at the end of my thirties, I was training for another marathon. I had Achilles tendonitis but kept running through it. The pain caused me to alter my gait significantly, but I powered through every run and muscled up every hill dictated by my training program, feeling so proud of myself for sticking to the plan. My opposite hip began to scream with the new stress I was placing on it. I was in almost constant pain. I ran until I could hardly walk, and then until I couldn't. Teaching was agony. I often cried in the car on the way to and home from school—from pain, from exhaustion, and in pity for myself. When I finally went to the doctor, I was immediately put on crutches and was told I needed an MRI because I likely had a stress fracture in my pelvis.

I kept running because I had been running and hustling for so long—trying to find an environment of touch that I could turn and return to, to finish my dissertation, then finish a book to get a job, a job which I hated, where I was under repetitive stress from embittered colleagues, and then needing to find another job, and then to write another book to receive tenure. I had developed a notion of myself, and not an uncommon one, that to make anything that I wanted to happen, I had to go at it like a person continually living in a montage. It's hard to stop when you've been raised on sports movie training montages and the "Just Do It" ethos of American hustle culture.

Throughout this handbook, I've leaned on repetition—its pleasures and possibilities, its uncanny ability to open out into difference, and its centrality to a resonant theory of running. On my writing desk is a yellow Post-it note with "REPETITION ITSELF CREATES BLISS" written in majuscule.[2] Below this quotation pulled from Barthes's *The Pleasure of the Text*, I have made an asterisk and written in all lowercase my response: "the reader finds pleasure in the text, the runner finds pleasure in the run. repetition can create bliss, but it can also create blisters, exhaustion, and stress fractures." I'm interested in what causes us to run ourselves into the ground, literally and metaphorically, and how we can avoid this so we can keep on running, in every sense of the word.

This is not a call to be more attuned to our bodies, or at least it is not only that. I want to think about how the repetitions in a practice, often performed alone, are also exercises built on the activation of things that come from elsewhere. The practices that animate our everyday lives are attempts to continue to stay in the grooves we've fallen into or efforts to create new grooves in which we want to slide, maybe grooves in which we think we might cruise more easily. These grooves could be friendship, love, writing, running, a job, a house, a child, a puppy—any desire for attachment could fit the bill. But stress too keeps us returning to these grooves, at pace, and with endurance. Toss

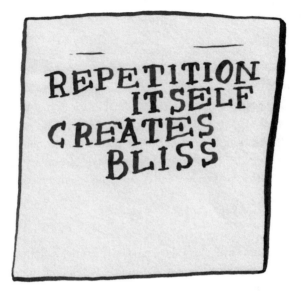

into the mix ambition, expectation, and the pressure to bend oneself into shapes of the preexisting world or the desire to resist them to make your own radically different spaces, and you can find yourself looping. This looping can tie you down too tightly, but it can also release you into a space that feels good. It's hard to know which, until you find yourself spinning with bliss, or simply spun out. Most of the time you're just in it.

In *Queer Phenomenology*, Sara Ahmed writes that compulsory heterosexuality is a repetitive stress injury that has hobbled our sense of the possible.[3] The libidinal ligatures that tied me to heterosexuality have been torn for a long time now, but they still hold so much of the world together, and their binds still haunt everyday life like ghost ligaments. It can wear you out to live with expectations, and it can grind you down resisting them too.

In the intervals of injury, days can feel fractured with the anxieties that running keeps at a distance. When I am injured, I lose my structure. I am forced to live in a new architecture of feeling—made of shuffled time, my healing body, and my hurt. This is a different kind of pain cave, one I've never learned to love, although I'm trying to learn to tolerate it better. I've been thinking about what this shuffled time can do. It can be time taken to rest, heal, reevaluate, and learn. Taking time can also expose the instability in linear time's surety. I want to say that in those moments we queer time, but that's only one possibility.

I want to move toward breaking down the fantasy of self-regulatory power. When my body breaks down or is injured from meeting the machinery of the world or from pounding myself against it, when I'm being cranked through the gears like Charlie Chaplin in *Modern Times*, or when I'm hitting the pavement at a force three times my body weight, as I am with each footfall when running, it is not only because I've participated in moving the gears and moving myself. I am also working in and with the things I'm coming up against and the things I'm moving toward. Like most of us living, I know that I sometimes do so at cross-purposes, that I engage in magical thinking, and that I can fall into a space of all-or-nothing scenarios. I can blame myself by taking full responsibility for running myself into the ground. And I can look for causes outside, by pointing to a job, a relationship, or an expectation that has run me ragged. I want to keep trying to approach the shuffled time of injury with more nuance, to take a step back and take in the vibrating structures in which we live, and the ways in which we lose and take time.

When I've taken time in a way that feels good, it has always been when I've allowed myself to live in queer temporality, when I've acquiesced to a break in the drive for production, achievement, and doing things at all costs. In these times, I've let my friends be my family, pick me up from the doctor, and walk my dog. I've lain on the couch, told and listened to stories, while drinking tea or whiskey, and I have let others' attachments to me and my attachments to them become a new feeling structure to hold me, a stretchy one of queer friendship, "of hapticality, or love."[4]

A Note on Cross-Training

Once I briefly took up boxing, thinking it could help give new balance to my running practice. I also imagined the class would allow me to hang out in a low-key way with people I wouldn't meet otherwise. When my friend Roxanne and I showed up at the gym, we learned that four out of six proto-boxers were university professors, like us. Another had a PhD but was no longer in academia, and the other was the father of a teenager who boxed in the class after us. He would box, she would box, then they would eat doughnuts and call it a Saturday.

I wanted to box because I was coming back from a hip injury that left me feeling weak and less confident in my body than I'm used to. I hoped the class would restore some of my strength and swagger. Jessi gave me silver boxing gloves for my birthday so I wouldn't have to slide my hands into someone else's sweaty mitts. And Roxanne gave me pink hand wraps so that I could have a bit of dandy flair underneath. For a while it was great to punch things in my silver-coated hands, like having little angry astronauts at the ends of my arms. Then at one session, as I was resting between circuit drills, the boxing instructor told me I had the posture of "someone much older." That statement hung over the rest of the class for me like miasma. *Much*. I wish had asked: "Like how much?"

What I took from her comment at the time was that I was stooped and brittle, falling toward the grave. Since this experience, I have learned to think of my corporeal presentation as a writer's posture, and I have embraced it. The boxing coach's intended slight sometimes crosses my mind when I'm running, as I'm feeling my breath "coaxing open a readerly concave chest," as the poet Lisa Robertson writes.[1] And as I swing my arms from heart to side, I smile and imagine myself out there in the future, still running, as someone much older.

Later I found out my friend Cait had taken a class with the same instructor, who had told them something similar. But Cait, my hero, said in response: "I wrote a book."[2] Damn, I wish I had thought of that.

In sum, I recommend swimming as cross-training.

A Note on Running to Music

The novelist Haruki Murakami espouses the pleasures of running to the Lovin' Spoonful on his Sony Walkman in his memoir *What I Talk about When I Talk about Running.*[1] Viv Albertine, guitarist from the punk band the Slits, listens to Kate Bush's *Hounds of Love* on her iPod when she runs in all the weathers that England can throw at her.[2] The philosopher Martha Nussbaum runs to the music in her head. She memorizes operas to "play" while she does her long training runs.[3]

For the last several years I stopped running with music when I run outside to try to listen to my breathing and footfall, the cadence of my run. Often, I forget myself and pay distracted attention instead to the sea and seabirds as I run along the ocean or to the trees swinging their rain-slicked boughs above my head and the crunching sticks and leaves below my feet when I run in the forest. I still listen to my little silver square MP3 music player with headphones if I run on a treadmill at a gym, particularly a hotel gym when I'm traveling, unless I want to

watch a murder show, Anderson Cooper, or Rachel Maddow on one of those little mounted personal televisions.

Running with or without music has become a polarizing practice in running circles. The writer Malcolm Gladwell thinks "it's soft to run with music." He believes people who run to music "are running from their running" because they find "the act of running so terrifying" that they need to be distracted from it. Gladwell thinks if you want to run with music, you "should be doing something else."[4] I've never been terrified of running (only of getting run over), but I have enjoyed the pleasure of bounding around Brooklyn to Lil' Kim, running in the Great Smoky Mountains to bluegrass banjos and old-time Appalachian music, and doing loops around the Sea Wall in Vancouver to the crescendos of Sigur Rós, especially on windy days when the surf is a little wild and I feel like I'm running through a Turner paining.

There's probably no bigger twit running than Malcolm Gladwell, who conceives of himself as one of the hardest bros out there. Still, his screed got me thinking. Running with softness is a lovely idea. Running with softness is doing the *something else* that Gladwell calls for, something other than what he is doing, which is what I always want to be doing. Running with softness can create an environment of touch that we can turn and return to. Running with softness can be a space of renewal, a space to be ourselves, a space of freedom. Running with softness can be done with or without music.

Big Gay 10K

A few years ago, I received an email from my ex-girlfriend Zoë with the subject line "San Francisco Big Gay 10K." There was an attachment showing an image of the race results, and a one-word message: "Ha!" The image showed Zoë's name just topping Tara's, another former love. At one time, briefly, they were rivals for my affection when we were all in DC and I lived in the queer punk house called the Pony House near Dupont Circle. My two ex-loves wouldn't have recognized each other by sight—they have never knowingly met—but they are aware of each other's names. The closeness of their names and times touches me, as does Zoë's delight in her slight edging out, years after we have all moved on to other relationships. The race results are a reminder of past desires and imperfect intimacies, and of the kind of romantic algebra that finds exes meeting each other when distance, space, and time are solved for in queer life. My ex-lovers ran through overlapping intensities and temporalities as they raced up and down the streets of San

Francisco without being aware of all the variables. This equation only came to light through running and the race volunteers' diligence, in the registering and collecting of the electronic timers that read the data of feet crossing lines: the math that runners make. When I read Zoë's email, I imagined those two crossing the line, recognizable to one another simply as runners; and, if only for a moment, elective affinities in New Balances.

This One's for the Rabbits, the Also-Rans, and the Dreamers

What we are learning, again and again, is that we cannot do this alone.

When the great Kenyan runner Eliud Kipchoge broke the two-hour mark by running 1:59:40 for the marathon distance in Vienna, Austria, in October 2019, he did so on a specially designed course with forty-one world-class runners working as pacemakers to help him do it. Some of these pacemakers, or rabbits, as they are sometimes called, were part of Kipchoge's regular training group from Kaptagat in the Kenyan highlands; they were already familiar with his cadence and style. Additional rabbits came from farther afield and learned on the job how to run together—three were brothers from Norway, while others were from Australia, Ethiopia, Japan, Switzerland, Turkey, Uganda, and the United States. All these runners were established stars of track and field, world champions, record holders, and Olympic medal winners in their own right, but on this day, they were also-rans. Their only ambition was to do their part in the intricate ballet that would enable Kipchoge to run the blistering, steady sub-4:34-mile pace he needed to break two hours.

Since almost no one can keep up the pace necessary to run the whole distance with Kipchoge, the rabbits were switched in and out in a highly choreographed manner at predetermined intervals. At any given time there were seven who ran in a unique Y formation around him. To picture the shape, imagine the inverse of how birds fly. The positioning of the runners was designed to funnel as much wind as possible away from Kipchoge, so he could run in the path of least resistance, in a little pocket tucked among the rabbits that had its own weather.

What Kipchoge did in the Ineos 1:59 Challenge in Vienna was amazing, but not surprising. He had already run a 2:01:40 in Berlin in 2018 for the official world marathon record and a 2:00:25 in 2017 in Nike's Breaking2 event held at Monza, the famous Formula One racetrack in Italy, where he raced against Zersenay Tadese and Lelissa Desisa in a similar event designed to run 26.2 miles in under two hours. With all the conditions engineered to being as close to perfect for running as possible, it was not hard to imagine that Kipchoge could shave off twenty-six seconds, just a hair more than a second per mile.

I turned on my computer to watch the attempt with a sense of the inevitable, even though I know from personal experience that anything can happen in a marathon. I felt too, like many other runners, that there was less heart in this event than in

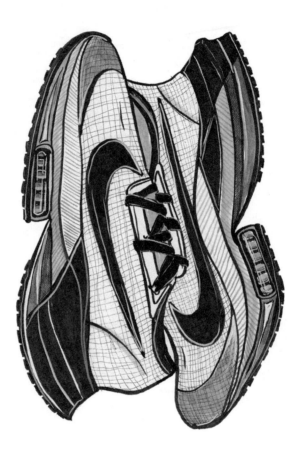

an open marathon race. Even before the start, as I watched the pre-run coverage, I was drifting around bored in a sea of experts in aerodynamics, nutritionists, timing technologies, and special carbon fiber shoes. The event was organized by the CEO of a huge chemical company, the richest man in Britain, who seemed to be able to throw unlimited money toward any small problem that emerged. I felt that the packaging of the event and its media coverage were drowning out everything I loved about running. For those of us who don't run for prizes or for our livelihoods, something else brings us to running; some indeterminate or unspecified thing pulls us toward the sport as a practice. What draws us and keeps us going can't be quantified or fully accounted for. I tuned in for the eventfulness of the attempt, but I was not expecting to find resonance with my love for running or to feel my fervor.

My plan had been to watch Kipchoge, but quickly my emotional investment shifted toward the pacemakers. Rabbits learn to read their bodies, and the bodies of the runners they pace. To be good at it involves an incredible sense of rhythm along with the desire and ability to stay attuned. Rabbits are experts in hapticality, in knowing what and who running touches. Kipchoge's rabbits were called up to run as perfectly as possible, to feel the road and the air for him, to hold him right where he needed to be. The pressure and the potential shame of messing this up, of tripping Kipchoge or another runner, of throwing the whole operation off seemed gargantuan. After each successful switchover of rabbits, I experienced a slight release of tension, a softening effect, like the way plot dissolves in a poet's novel, carrying the reader along with the form and rhythm of language.

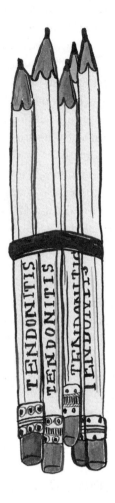

As I watched the runners speed down the road in Vienna, Kipchoge in an all-white kit, surrounded by his pacers in all black, I found myself moved by the grace of their bodies moving in sync. I was touched by their running, and this feeling lifted me out of myself. Even my thinking fell into a new cadence. For the time it took for the rabbits to deliver Kipchoge to the point where he knew he would finish in time, all my disappointments with my own running, with my body, with my collection of tendonitises and wonky knee were pushed somewhere else.

I was relieved to discover that sometimes even the most artificial conditions can't kill what running touches in me. A good feeling cracked open when Kipchoge smiled, spread out his arms, and crossed the line, but what really did me in was the pacemakers coming in behind him, after letting him go the last three hundred meters alone. At the end, the rabbits were still full of running, their bodies visibly overflowing with joy, in the pink of their lives, in their pink Nike VaporFlys.

Loops—Practice—Repetition—Ritual

A running loop starts from one place (often, but not always, home) and stretches out a distance only to bring you back to where you began. The repetitive act of running regular loops is a tracing of the familiar that changes or deepens. You change, becoming faster or slower, depending on your fitness or mood, the day, the year, the weather; and places change too, with the seasons, gentrification, nature taking over, erosion, fire, water, politics, and pandemics. Stay with a run long enough or do a loop often enough and this act of tracing opens up a meditative zone and a space for feeling that is beyond the thrill of the new.

Loops are repetitions that stretch out into practices of touching, feeling, and the slow accrual of knowing. A loop you know well is a route you coast along guided by muscle memory, but what will cross your runner-brain in practice, you never know. You can't run for a long time without thinking about time itself. This kind of thinking can focus on pace, distance, and estimated time of arrival back at the start. But running a long time lends itself to thinking about time that isn't linear, the time of memory. On your familiar loops, it is easy to lap yourself. The experience can throw you, but it can also allow for a moment of recognition and a chance to give a subtle runner's nod to memory and keep on moving.

Loops can also be scissory things, tools to slice open the twine of responsibilities that tie the day together too tightly. They can bring you to a point of tension and then snip it so you can unwind a little. Loops can also form a fastening, handle, or catch, something you can grab and hang on to when you need it. Loops are versatile, but they are not dialectical: they are practices of tough and tender circulation.

When I lived in Buffalo, working a job I hated in a department with hostile colleagues and little hope that I would be able to leave the situation I was in, my running loops helped me to hang in there. I would often run past the hotel where Michel Foucault stayed when he was a visiting professor at SUNY-Buffalo. Running helped lift me out of my malaise, at least for a little while. This "queer, theory loop," as I thought of it, often sparked thoughts of possibility, and of the beautiful formlessness of friendship as a way of life. I would imagine Foucault in his room, or down at the hotel bar, rereading his friend Roland Barthes's *S/Z*, a book, at its heart, about repetition and practice. I'd think of Foucault thinking about Barthes, about teaching, leaving Buffalo, going to Morocco, or at least to France.[1]

When I lived in Brooklyn, I would often do a five-mile run that I thought of as my "*Just Kids* loop." This route had me running from my apartment in Bushwick to the building near

Pratt where Patti Smith and Robert Mapplethorpe lived together and made art when they were young.[2] I would run up the short stack of stairs and touch the dark red door, attempting to make contact with the complicated and deep love that once filled that apartment. The physical touching of the door was important; it was what transformed the run into a ritual. When I put my hand to the door, I felt a queer connection through time, the never fully defined ways people can touch each other through art, style, and personality, what Julietta Singh calls "the transformative touch between friends . . . that cannot be reduced to the normative cultural paradigms," and what Stefano Harney and Fred Moten call "hapticality, or love."[3]

I have a lifelong habit of creating loops like this. Now one of my most regular routes has me setting out from my apartment and quickly running by the Memorial to the Sex Workers of the West End of Vancouver. A couple of miles later, I pass the statue of the great sprinter Harry Jerome, who racked up a total of seven world records in the course of his career, running for Canada and for the University of Oregon, where he liked to turn his sweatshirt inside out so that the letters faintly spelled "nogero." This flipping was a small act of rebellion against the racism he faced both in Eugene and at home. Every time I reach Harry Jerome's statue, I engage in a little ritual where I run up the hill from the path to touch his leg, the leg where he tore a hole in his quadriceps while running his heart out for the Canada that then called him "arrogant" and "lazy," and I say out loud: "Looking good, Harry!" And he does, caught in a tape-breaking stretch, perpetually extending himself, like an athlete, like a lover.

Touching Jerome's leg always gives me a little boost as I continue around the Sea Wall that belts Stanley Park. I finish up at Sunset Beach, where there is often a group of fit shirtless men doing squats and push-ups in front of the AIDS memorial, which is the most fitting tribute I can think of for those lost in that pandemic. This loop, following Elizabeth Freeman, is "a queer hauntological exercise," reminding me of the way queer time can feel out of step with normative time, and how much of queer memory is also a memorial for things lost.[4] My West End loop is heavy with loss, like all spaces once you really get to know them, but it's also a runner's dream that takes me along the Pacific Ocean, through and around old-growth forest, and with a superabundance of mountains in almost every direction in the distance.

Cooldown and Stretching

Running and writing are the only sustained practices I've kept nearly all my life. Like most people who are drawn to long-distance running and to writing, I share a dogged passion for discipline, a high tolerance for pain and disappointment, a desire to endure endurance projects, and a longing to get to the ends of things—trails, races, ideas, essays, books, what my body can do—to find myself spent at last with miles logged or words on the page.[1] I make an effort to get myself to my writing desk regularly, herding paragraphs like a border collie in high spirits. And like most runners who have been at it a long time, I want to get out the door nearly every day, and for longer on Sundays. I take special care with punctuation and grammar, my tenses and Achilles tendons, hip flexors and hamstrings. I do these things because I love the shapes of runners and sentences, for the feeling of when form falls into place and words and miles flow easily, and I do it for the pleasure of pushing my body and brain to see what happens.

I love these practices for their capaciousness, the way they take me to zones of thinking and feeling that surprise me. When I set out on a run, I can never be completely sure of the turns the weather will take, what my body will feel like, who or what I might find out there. Before I sit down at my desk, I never know what memories will arise, how and when an idea will come, or what syllables it will wear when it does. I love writing and running when they are easy (which is seldom), and I keep doing them even when they are difficult or when I feel hangdog and lazy because I've learned that that is where the ease comes from. And when it fails to come, I can still feel good about giving my effort to these practices, even when I'm terrible or mediocre at them, because I think they are beautiful and worthwhile in and of themselves. I keep practicing because I want to remain a writer and a runner, to touch these worlds, to help stretch them in my own small way, and to continue to be stretched by them.

I love writing and running, even when these things break my heart, which is often. Like most runners, I have been hampered by injuries that have prevented me from running for stretches of time—Achilles tendonitis, a deranged right meniscus, plantar fasciitis, sprained ankles, stress fractures, and a mysterious hip injury have all kept me on the couch and in the physiotherapist's office on and off for years. During these more stationary periods, I found that I wasn't able to write much or well, and that running and writing are intimately tangled for me. When I'm not able to lace up my running shoes and head out for a while or spend time pushing paragraphs around, I can feel lost and lethargic. I become irritable, unexpressive, not the best version of myself. I've learned over time that injury and interruptions to writing and running well are sometimes unavoidable, and that rest and fallow periods are not a break from these practices; they are inevitable. This knowledge does not always make me less grumpy or more pleasant to be around, but if I can let myself know it, avoid obsessing over how I ended up where I am, and instead turn my focus to recovery, I can convince myself that if I stop for a moment or even a few months, I won't lose everything, and I will be able to go again. In my better moments, I realize that even if I can't run or write again, I won't lose everything, that I have other things that give my life meaning and pleasure. And I know one day I will take my last run and write my final good sentence, and this too gives my practices meaning.

We reproduce ourselves each day through the repetitive things we do, and even though they are often similar, each day, each run, and each new sentence written has the potential to shift things—a person, a thought, an afternoon—if only slightly. Over time these shifts are part of what forms a self, a body, and a body of work. While bodies and bodies of work are wonderful things, often how we appear to the world and how worlds come to meet us, this handbook is ultimately about the beauty of practice, the often unseen and overlooked actions of trying to do something well because you love it, and because by doing so you can touch and be touched by others who love it too.

Vade mecum.

Introduction

1 The term *personal record*, or *PR*, is also frequently used. My initiation into running came with the term *personal best*, so it remains at the forefront in the glossary of my running memories.

2 An "ultra" refers to an ultramarathon, which is anything over the standard marathon length of 26.2 miles. In a "backyard ultra" runners must consecutively run the distance of 4.1666666 miles in less than one hour. A loop of this distance must be repeated every hour to stay in the contest. The distance is measured in this way so that any runner who completes twenty-four laps has run 100 miles in one day. "Last man standing" refers to the rule that the race is not over until all the competitors or all the competitors minus one have failed to complete the distance in the time allotted or have dropped out. If no runner outlasts another, then all competitors receive the distinction of "DNF," or "did not finish," and there is no winner.

3 This is not to say that freedom from pronouns and peer review is always desirable. Constraints can be lovely. Peer review can

be immensely helpful; it can give you things that can help shift your thinking and writing. And pronouns, too, are stretchy and stretchable constraints that do a lot for an identity moving in a world. Here, I only wish to say that I think sometimes a space where identity is on the move and thinking and feeling are un-fixed, at least for a while, can be a wonderful thing.

4 Soon after I wrote this paragraph, I read the introduction to Maggie Nelson's *On Freedom*, where she asks: "Can you think of a more depleted, imprecise, or weaponized word?" (3). This question zipped right through me because I'm not sure I can. But also because, like Nelson, I think it is still worth thinking with, and sometimes it is the only word that feels right.

5 Running handbooks that could be found in my childhood home: Fixx, *Complete Book of Running*; Rohé, *Zen of Running*; Shee-han, *Running and Being*; and Spino, *Beyond Jogging*.

6 Murakami, *What I Talk about When I Talk about Running*, vii.

7 There are lots of models of writers working in this mode. I'm par-ticularly moved by the way Ann Cvetkovich uses this strategy. She puts it thus: "The memoir also functions as a research method because it reveals the places where feeling and lived experience collide with academic training and critique." In *Depression*, 80.

8 Barthes was no stranger to writing about sports; two of his best-known "mythologies" are about the semiotics of compe-tition and performance in the Tour de France and in amateur wrestling. See "In the Ring," 3–14; "Tour de France as Epic," 122–33. Barthes also wrote the text for a documentary film for the Canadian Broadcasting Company directed by Hubert Aquin called *What Is Sport?* that was then published as a book. In this slim volume, he extends his reading of sport outside of France to include meditations on the relationship of five sports, which are matched to five national cultures, including bullfighting in

Spain, car racing in the United States, cycling in France, hockey in Canada, and soccer in England.

9   Barthes, *Lover's Discourse*, 4.

10 Shepard, *Living Mountain*, xliii.

11 Harney and Moten, *Undercommons*, 98.

12 Foucault, "Friendship as a Way of Life," 135–40.

13 Berlant, "Love, a Queer Feeling," 439.

14 "Runner-brain" comes from Sillitoe's novella *The Loneliness of the Long-Distance Runner*.

15 Barthes, *Neutral*, on "baffling paradigms" (6) and on stretching as a form (197).

On the Subversive Nature of This Handbook

1   Deloria, *Playing Indian*.

2   Barthes, *Lover's Discourse*, 136.

3   Baudrillard's disgust with running in the United States can be found in multiple texts, most notably *America*, 20, 38–39; but also in *Simulacra and Simulation*, 13; and "Operational White-wash," 44–50.

4   Ullyot, *Running Free*, 10.

5   For more on the story of the cover, see Metzler, "Iconic and Ironic."

6   Fixx, *Complete Book of Running*, xv.

7   Fixx, *Complete Book of Running*, 11.

8   Foucault, "Friendship as a Way of Life," 137.

A Note on "Just Do It"

1   Norman Mailer wrote extensively about Gilmore in his Pulitzer Prize–winning book *The Executioner's Song*.

2   Nike's "Just Do It" ad campaign makes me think of Walter Benjamin's famous assertion from "Theses on the Philosophy of History": "There is no document of culture which is not at the same time a document of barbarism. And just as such a document is not free of barbarism, barbarism taints also the manner in which it was transmitted from one owner to another" (256).

3   See the documentary film *Art & Copy* directed by Doug Pray, and also see Bella, "'Just Do It.'"

4   The Swoosh was designed by Katherine Davidson for Nike. Its shape is intended to indicate movement.

Leaving It All on the Track

1   Parker, "Once a Runner," 20.

2   My record in the 800 meters at Wofford College has been surpassed, but I might still hold the best time for the mile at West View Middle School. My mother ran into Coach Skeen, now retired, who told her that she thought I still held the record. To find out, I emailed the current track coach. She told me the best time they have recorded for the mile is a 6:01, but that their records only go back to 2011. I ran a 5:59 in 1991, so there's a twenty-year gap where someone might have eclipsed me. A sub-six mile is no big deal, considering that Diane Leather ran a 4:59 in 1954 and the current world record for the women's mile is 4:12, held by Sifan Hassan of the Netherlands. Still, I wish I could run that now.

3   My thinking about leaving "it" was influenced by Blanchfield's "On the Leave," 65–70. Jessi Jackson brought my attention to Joseph Roach's *It*, a book that thinks through the hard-to-define quality of "*it*" that "abnormally interesting people" (1), particularly celebrities, possess. While I don't put myself in that category, the idea that a kind of "it-ness" can result from, as Roach writes, "the

fortuitous convergence of personality and extraordinary circumstances or efforts" (8) rings true here.

Running Is a Contact Sport

1 BBC, "London Marathon 1981 and 1982 BBC Video part 1," excerpted, YouTube, posted March 13, 2015, https://www.youtube.com/watch?v=OAtw6krxDsA&t=1450s.

2 André Gide from the novel *Cahiers de la petite dame*, quoted in Barthes's discussion of the form of "stretching" in *Neutral*, 197.

3 Fixx, *Complete Book of Running*, 33.

4 Oates, "On Boxing."

Running after Olympians

1 Stewart and Berlant, "Couplets," 202.

2 Wrack, "'You Can't Win without Gay Players.'"

3 Murdoch, "Stars of Track and Field." See also Bentler, *Belle and Sebastian: If You're Feeling Sinister*.

4 At the time of this writing, the official world record for the marathon is 2:01:39, held by Eliud Kipchoge of Kenya, who set it at the Berlin Marathon in 2018.

5 Browning's poem fails to capture just how full of running Pheidippides was. The 25-mile run was done just days after he had run 150 miles to ask for help from the Spartans when the Persians first arrived in the city of Marathon. He had run 175 miles in just three days. And because he was a messenger, we can assume that this was not the first of his long-distance runs, only the last of many. Browning's poem inspired the founders of the modern Olympic games to create a race of 25 miles called the marathon, which was first run for men in 1896. The women's

marathon was not held in the Olympics until nearly a hundred years later, in 1984.

6 Kelly, "Running towards My Father."

7 Didion, "On Keeping a Notebook," 83.

Running Is Your Life

1 Lasse Virén was part of the second generation of talented Finnish runners from the 1970s. The first generation of "Flying Finns" is attributed to runners from the earlier twentieth century, especially Paavo Nurmi, who won nine Olympic gold medals and three silver ones. Virén won four Olympic gold medals in the 5,000- and 10,000-meter distances, winning both events in 1972 in Munich and in 1976 in Montreal.

Personal Best

1 The last time the pentathlon was an official competition in the Olympic Games was in 1980. It has since been replaced by the heptathlon, which has seven events: the 100-meter hurdles, high jump, shot put, 200 meters, long jump, javelin throw, and 800 meters.

2 Pat Donnelly also served as a technical adviser on *Personal Best*. She went on to help train Billy Crudup for his role as Steve Prefontaine in Towne's later film about running, *Without Limits*.

3 Barthes, *Lover's Discourse*, 224.

4 Carson, *Eros, the Bittersweet*, xi.

In Training for the Boston Marathon

1 Asics began as Onitsuku Tiger in 1949 in Kobe, Japan. The company name is an acronym that stands for the Latin maxim *anima sana in corpore sano*, meaning "sound mind, sound body." In

1977, the company switched to using Asics as the official brand name while still selling some heritage models under the original Onitsuku Tiger label.

Running the Risk Of

1   This thinking is inspired by J. Robert Oppenheimer, who after my years of writing about nuclear culture is always in my brain. See Oppenheimer, *Atom and Void*, 31.

Courage, or The Paris Marathon

1   In the course of writing this handbook, I learned that joggling is an established competitive sport. According to Wikipedia, "Jogglers say that the arm motions of juggling with three objects feels natural with the action and pace of jogging." "Joggling," Wikipedia, last edited May 30, 2022, https://en.wikipedia.org /wiki/Joggling.

2   McWilliams, "On the Road."

3   I was thinking about the relationship between field notes and storytelling in a general sense here, but also specifically Michael Taussig's *I Swear I Saw This* was on my mind as I was writing this section.

4   They are sometimes called "space blankets" because they were invented by NASA in 1964.

Runner's High

1   Barthes, *Lover's Discourse*, 11.

2   Henderson, *Long Slow Distance*, 8.

3   Henderson, *Long Slow Distance*, 8; see also his follow-up book, *Run Gently, Run Long*.

Let's Let Our Running Be Real

1   According to Csikszentmihalyi, "flow" is a state of absolute absorption with what you are doing that hits unexpectedly when you rise to a challenge that is just at your ability to meet it. If you're not up to the challenge, flow is impossible. And if the challenge is not enough of a challenge for your skill level, flow is likewise impossible. In sports, the concept of flow is connected with the experience of an athlete's optimum performance. For more about flow, see Csikszentmihalyi, *Flow*, as well as Jackson and Csikszentmihalyi, *Flow in Sports*.

2   Strasser and Becklund, *Swoosh*, 226.

3   Gardner, *Poverty Creek Journal*, 49.

4   Rohé, *Zen of Running*, n.p.

5   Berlant, *Desire/Love*, 5.

6   Barthes, *Lover's Discourse*, 22.

On Hitting the Wall and Writer's Block

1   Andersen-Schiess has said that she felt an extra pressure to finish the race because it was the first time women could run the marathon distance in the Olympic games. Prior to 1984 the longest distance available for athletes competing under the category of women was the 1,500 meters. Olympics, "An Unforgettable Marathon Finish—Gabriela Andersen-Schiess | Olympic Rewind," YouTube, posted December 6, 2004, https://www.youtube.com/watch?v=lBasZWjd92k.

Repetitive Stress

1   Lewis, "Lonely Marathon," 42.

2   Barthes, *Pleasure of the Text*, 41.

3 Ahmed, *Queer Phenomenology*, 91.

4 Harney and Moten, *Undercommons*, 97.

A Note on Cross-Training

1 Robertson, *Baudelaire Fractal*, 17. Robertson's book is also concerned with writing, aging, and what a body can do.

2 See McKinney's book *Information Activism*, which focuses on approaches to data and accessibility in media spaces wielded by queer and feminist social activists.

A Note on Running to Music

1 Murakami, *What I Talk about When I Talk about Running*, 4.

2 Albertine waxes enthusiastic on her running practice in her memoir *Clothes, Clothes, Clothes. Music, Music, Music. Boys, Boys, Boys*, 306.

3 Nussbaum, "'Where the Dark Feelings Hold Sway,'" 181.

4 Crane, "Eight of Our Favorite Writers on Why They Run."

Loops—Practice—Repetition—Ritual

1 This flight of fantasy is driven first by the fact that when I lived in Buffalo, every first get-to-know-you chat included, "Let me show you the hotel where Foucault lived when he was here." Second, it was embellished by Foucault's letter to Barthes dated February 28, 1970, which reads: "Thank you, dear Roland, for sending me your *S/Z*. I've just read it in one sitting. It is magnificent, the first true analysis of text that I've ever read. I'm leaving for America—Buffalo, where I must, in two months, teach 'French Literature.' I'm taking *S/Z*, which I'll assign to the students as a basic text. And we'll get some practice. Morocco? Will I see you

when I return in May? Yours, dear Roland, in friendship and admiration, M. Foucault." See Foucault, untitled letter to Roland Barthes, in *Album*, 198. On the "formlessness" of friendship, see Foucault, "Friendship as a Way of Life," 136.

2 Smith, *Just Kids*.

3 Singh, *No Archive Will Restore You*, 105; Harney and Moten, *Undercommons*, 97–99.

4 Freeman, *Time Binds*, 13.

Cooldown and Stretching

1 Spinoza, *Ethics*, 87. The Spinozan prod of "what a body can do" can never be answered because bodies are always changing as the world changes and bodies move to meet it—or represent it, or stretch out for it—but this doesn't stop me from trying to find out what *my* body can do.

BIBLIOGRAPHY

THINGS I THOUGHT WITH, THINGS I RAN WITH

Films

Bentler, R. J. Director. *Belle and Sebastian: If You're Feeling Sinister*. PitchforkTV, 2013.

Cramer, John L. Narration editor and narrator. *Running Is Your Life*. Sports Video. Woodland Hills, CA, 1980. https://www.youtube.com /watch?v=r-LWqJPs-sA.

Hudson, Hugh. Director. *Chariots of Fire*. Twentieth Century Fox, 1981.

Pray, Doug. Director. *Art & Copy*. Art & Industry, 2009.

Scott, Jake. Director. *Kipchoge: The Last Milestone*. Ridley Scott Creative Group, 2021.

Stallone, Sylvester. Director. *Rocky IV*. MGM/UA Entertainment Company, 1985.

Towne, Robert. Director. *Personal Best*. Warner Brothers, 1982.

Towne, Robert. Director. *Without Limits*. Warner Brothers, 1998.

Music

Murdoch, Stuart. Songwriter. "The Stars of Track and Field." On the album Belle & Sebastian, *If You're Feeling Sinister*. Sony Music, 1996.

Team Dresch. *Personal Best*. Joint release by Candyass Records and Chainsaw Records, both of Portland, Oregon, 1995.

Television

BBC. "London Marathon 1981 and 1982 BBC Video part 1." Excerpted. YouTube, posted March 13, 2015. https://www.youtube.com/watch?v=OAtw6krxDsA&t=1450s.

DeGeneres, Ellen. "The Puppy Episode." *Ellen*. ABC. April 30, 1997.

Texts

Ahmed, Sara. *Queer Phenomenology*. Durham, NC: Duke University Press, 2006.

Albertine, Viv. *Clothes, Clothes, Clothes. Music, Music, Music. Boys, Boys, Boys*. New York: St. Martin's Press, 2014.

Barthes, Roland. *Camera Lucida*. Translated by Richard Howard. New York: Hill and Wang, 1980.

Barthes, Roland. "In the Ring." In *Mythologies*, translated by Richard Howard and Annette Lavers, 3–14. New York: Hill and Wang, 2003.

Barthes, Roland. *A Lover's Discourse: Fragments*. Translated by Richard Howard. New York: Hill and Wang, 1978.

Barthes, Roland. *The Neutral*. Translated by Rosalind E. Krauss and Denis Hollier. New York: Columbia University Press, 2005.

Barthes, Roland. *The Pleasure of the Text*. Translated by Richard Miller. New York: Hill and Wang, 1975.

Barthes, Roland. "The Tour de France as Epic." In *Mythologies*, translated by Richard Howard and Annette Lavers, 122–33. New York: Hill and Wang, 2003.

Barthes, Roland. *What Is Sport?* Translated by Richard Howard. New Haven, CT: Yale University Press, 2007.

Baudrillard, Jean. *America*. Translated by Chris Turner. New York: Verso, 1988.

Baudrillard, Jean. "Operational Whitewash." In *The Transparency of Evil: Essays on Extreme Phenomena*, translated by James Benedict, 44–50. New York: Verso, 2009.

Baudrillard, Jean. *Simulacra and Simulation*. Translated by Sheila Faria Glaser. Ann Arbor: University of Michigan Press, 1994.

Bella, Timothy. "'Just Do It': The Surprising and Morbid Origin Story of Nike's Slogan." *Washington Post*, April 4, 2018.

Benjamin, Walter. "Theses on the Philosophy of History." In *Illuminations*, translated by Harry Zohn, 253–64. New York: Harcourt Brace Jovanovich, 1968.

Berlant, Lauren. *Desire/Love*. Brooklyn: Punctum Books, 2012.

Berlant, Lauren. "Love, a Queer Feeling." In *Homosexuality and Psychoanalysis*, edited by Tim Dean and Christopher Lane, 432–51. Chicago: University of Chicago Press, 2001.

Blanchfield, Brian. "On the Leave." In *Proxies*, 65–70. New York: Nightboat, 2016.

Carson, Anne. *Eros, the Bittersweet*. Funks Grove, IL: Dalkey Archive Press, 1998.

Crane, Bent. "Eight of Our Favorite Writers on Why They Run." *Outside*, June 26, 2017. https://www.outsideonline.com/health/running/our-favorite-writers-why-they-run/.

Csikszentmihalyi, Mihaly. *Flow: The Psychology of Optimal Experience*. New York: Harper and Row, 1990.

Cvetkovich, Ann. *Depression: A Public Feeling*. Durham, NC: Duke University Press, 2012.

Deloria, Philip. *Playing Indian*. New Haven, CT: Yale University Press, 1999.

Didion, Joan. "On Keeping a Notebook." In *Slouching towards Bethlehem*, 73–83. New York: Farrar, Straus and Giroux, 1966.

Fixx, James. *The Complete Book of Running*. New York: Random House, 1977.

Foucault, Michel. "Friendship as a Way of Life." Interview with R. de Ceccaty, J. Danet, and J. Le Bitoux. Translated by John Johnson. In *Essential Works of Foucault*, vol. 1, *1954—1984: Ethics, Subjectivity and Truth*, edited by Paul Rabinow, 135–40. New York: New Press, 1997.

Foucault, Michel. Untitled letter to Roland Barthes. In *Barthes Album: Unpublished Correspondences and Texts*, translated by Jody Gladding, 198. New York: Columbia University Press, 2019.

Freeman, Elizabeth. *Time Binds: Queer Temporalities, Queer Histories*. Durham, NC: Duke University Press, 2010.

Gardner, Thomas. *Poverty Creek Journal*. North Adams, MA: Tupelo, 2014.

Harney, Stefano, and Fred Moten. *The Undercommons: Fugitive Planning and Black Study*. Brooklyn: Minor Compositions, 2013.

Henderson, Joe. *Long Slow Distance: The Humane Way to Train*. Bolton, ON: Amazon.com, 2010. Originally published in 1969 by Tafnews Press.

Henderson, Joe. *Run Gently, Run Long*. Mountain View, CA: Anderson World, 1974.

Jackson, Susan, and Mihaly Csikszentmihalyi. *Flow in Sports: The Keys to Optimal Experiences and Performances*. Windsor, ON: Human Kinetics, 1999.

Kelly, Devin Gael. "Running towards My Father: On Marathons, Perfection, and the Impossibility of Intimacy." *Literary Hub*, June 16, 2017. https://lithub.com/running-towards-my-father/.

Lewis, Kevin. "The Lonely Marathon." *Theology Today* 39, no. 1 (1982): 39–45.

Mailer, Norman. *The Executioner's Song*. New York: Little, Brown, 1979.

McKinney, Cait. *Information Activism: A Queer History of Lesbian Media Technologies*. Durham, NC: Duke University Press, 2020.

McWilliams, James. "On the Road." *Paris Review*, April 16, 2018. https://www.theparisreview.org/blog/2016/04/18/on-the-road/.

Metzler, Brian. "Iconic and Ironic." *Runner's World*, March 23, 2012. https://www.runnersworld.com/advanced/a20849442/iconic-and-ironic/.

Murakami, Haruki. *What I Talk about When I Talk about Running*. Translated by Philip Gabriel. New York: Vintage, 2008.

Nelson, Maggie. *On Freedom*. New York: McClelland and Stewart, 2021.

Nussbaum, Martha C. "'Where the Dark Feelings Hold Sway': Running to Music." In *Running and Philosophy: A Marathon for the Mind*, edited by Michael W. Austin, 181–92. Malden, MA: Blackwell, 2007.

Oates, Joyce Carol. "On Boxing." *New York Times*, June 16, 1985.

Oppenheimer, J. Robert. *Atom and Void: Essays on Science and Community*. Princeton, NJ: Princeton University Press, 2014.

Parker, John L., Jr. "Once a Runner." In *The Runner's Literary Companion*, edited by Garth Battista, 1–22. New York: Penguin, 1994.

Roach, Joseph. *It*. Ann Arbor: University of Michigan Press, 2007.

Robertson, Lisa. *The Baudelaire Fractal*. Toronto: Coach House Books, 2020.

Rohé, Fred. *The Zen of Running*. Middletown, CA: Organic Marketing, 1974.

Sheehan, George. *Running and Being*. New York: Rodale Books, 1978.

Shepard, Nan. *The Living Mountain*. Edinburgh: Canongate, 2011.

Sillitoe, Alan. *The Loneliness of the Long-Distance Runner*. New York: Signet, 1959.

Singh, Julietta. *No Archive Will Restore You*. Goleta, CA: Punctum Books, 2018.

Smith, Patti. *Just Kids*. New York: Ecco, 2010.

Spino, Mike. *Beyond Jogging: The Innerspaces of Running*. Milbrae, CA: Celestial Arts, 1976.

Spinoza, Benedict. *Ethics: On the Correction of Understanding*. Translated by Andrew Boyle. London: Everyman's Library, 1959.

Stewart, Kathleen, and Lauren Berlant. "Couplets." *Women and Performance: a journal of feminist theory* 29, no. 3 (2019): 199–210.

Strasser, J. B., and Laurie Becklund. *Swoosh: The Unauthorized Story of Nike and the Men Who Played There*. New York: HarperCollins, 1993.

Taussig, Michael. *I Swear I Saw This: Drawings in Fieldwork Notebooks, Namely My Own*. Chicago: University of Chicago Press, 2011.

Ullyot, Joan L. *Running Free: A Guide for Women Runners and Their Friends*. New York: G. P. Putnam's Sons, 1980.

Wrack, Suzanne. "'You Can't Win without Gay Players,' Says USA's World Cup Hero Megan Rapinoe." *Guardian*, June 28, 2019.